Dance Studio TRANSFORMATION

Build A 7-Figure Studio,
Increase Your Community Impact And
GET BACK YOUR LIFE

CLINT SALTER

Published by Clint Salter Pty Ltd
Dance Studio Owners Association
hello@dancestudioownersassociation.com
www.dancestudioownersassociation.com

National Library of Australia Cataloguing-in-Publication entry

Creator: Salter, Clint, author.

Title: Dance studio transformation : build a 7-figure studio, increase your community impact and get back your life! / Clint Salter.

ISBN: 9780994561008 (paperback)

Notes: Includes bibliographical references.

Subjects: Dance schools--Business management.
Business enterprises--Australia.
Success in business--Australia.
Self-realization.

Dewey Number: 658.401

Dedicated to my best friend and mother, Kim Salter. Without your continual love and support, this book would not have been written.

CONTENTS

Preface...

OR AS I LIKE TO CALL IT, THE BEGINNING

Was it jumping out of a trash can in a grey unitard when I was nine years old, dancing to Alley Cat, that made me want to have dance in my life forever? Well, no... but it certainly made for a great photo to show at my 30th birthday party!

From the day my friends dragged me away from choir at school, suggesting I join dance group instead, I was hooked. I knew I was at home as soon as I walked into that dance room. There are no words to describe how I felt during those first few classes, allowing my body to move to the music. I'll never forget that feeling. Since that day, I've never looked back. And I'm so glad I didn't, for if dance hadn't played such a major role in my life, I wouldn't be the person I am today.

From dancer to dance teacher to dance studio owner... This was my journey to owning my own studio, and it may well be one you're familiar with. Can you remember how you felt the moment the idea of owning your own studio popped into your head? The moment you realized that you could have your own business, your own studio? Did you get goosebumps born from pure excitement at the thought of being able to make a living out of doing something you love, and having the freedom of working for yourself?

I know that's what I thought at the age of 16, when a dance mom suggested that I could open my own dance studio. Admittedly, my first reaction was, 'Are you crazy, lady?' But then that quickly turned to excitement as I considered the possibilities that lay ahead.

Many of us jump in headfirst when we start our studio. From the time we have our logo designed to the moment we cut the opening ribbon, our heart and soul is poured into every part of the process. We give everything we have, and yet, there are so many studio owners whose businesses are merely surviving, or to be brutally honest, dying. Why? How can one studio a few blocks away be bursting with students and thriving on all levels, and another be simply plodding along at the same pace, or worse, sinking?

We're extremely lucky to be a part of an industry that has seen such rapid growth over the last ten years. These days, dance is truly in the spotlight globally! There have never been more television shows, films, books, magazines, programs and websites based on dance than there are today, and it's nothing short of exciting.

This dance boom has meant that more people are becoming aware of dance classes and wanting to be a part of the magic, and it's important that you're aware of this prime opportunity so that you can act fast and ensure you become the 'go to' studio in your area sooner rather than later. It's about having a solid business model and automated administration system in place to support hundreds of students, recruiting knowledgeable, responsible and passionate teachers, and having a strategic and scheduled student attraction and retention plan in place. These three things alone allow you to spend more time working *on* rather than *in* the business, which means your stress levels plummet and you get to enjoy a life outside of the studio while making a great living. Imagine that!

The main problem I come across continually – having worked in this space for the past 22 years and closely with studio owners for the past seven – is that studio owners are standing still and not moving forward because you're confused. Confused about how to effectively make the transition from where you are currently, to your goal of becoming a 'go to' studio.

You may feel overwhelmed and unsure of how to go about getting new student leads through the door and keeping them there without it chewing up all their time and your bank balance. Or maybe you're stuck in an admin trap and feel like you can never get your head above water. Or perhaps you feel like you're wearing all the hats in your business, but you know that if you want to grow, you can't continue working this way.

I'm happy to tell you that you don't have to keep operating this way and there is a light at the end of the tunnel. I'm sure you'll agree that the rules of owning and growing a dance studio have changed dramatically over the last few years. But there are a few things you have to stop doing immediately if you want to transform your studio and go to the next level. Every day, I speak with studio owner after studio owner, each of them doing all the administration work themselves using a class fee model that undervalues their services and sends them broke due to all their discounts and unlimited class pricing models. On top of that, they are executing reactive marketing campaigns and still using newspaper advertising to try and generate leads.

But times have changed. Technology alone has greatly impacted the way you need to do business, and you must embrace this if you want to still have your studio a month, a year or 40 years from today. Marshall Goldsmith wrote a great book called *What Got You Here, Won't Get You There*, which looks at why so many people, despite their intelligence and wealth, don't make it to the top of the ladder and end up just treading water. In this book, I'm going to share with you an action plan for climbing that ladder to business and personal success.

I speak with over 12,000 studio owners each week through our podcast, newsletter, training and programs. I see inside hundreds of studios around the globe daily and while some have the recipe for studio success, many don't. That's about to change.

Dance Studio Transformation is here to help you build that dream studio you have always wanted, while you make a bigger impact in the lives of your local dance families. It's also about giving you back your life! I know, right... A life outside the walls of the studio. That's something that many studio owners don't believe is attainable, but I'm here to tell you it is – and more importantly, I can show you how you can get that freedom.

Whether you're about to start on your journey of being a studio owner or have been at it for years, whether you're struggling to get your head out of the water or have a highly profitable studio... This book is for you. I've created a playbook to show you step by step how you can become the 'go to' studio in your area. I've laid it all out in the upcoming chapters so that you can take the strategies and tactics and then run with them. Yes – your studio's transformation is in your hands as implementing the ideas in the book is all up to you!

The sad truth is that I know only 10% of people who have this book will read the whole thing and out of those people, 10% will actually execute the ideas here in your hot little hands. I hope you're in that small group! Because there is absolutely no reason you can't be, aside from your hunger and commitment to building a 'go to' studio.

Thank you for taking this journey with me. I'm excited for you to jump in, to learn, to make positive changes in your studio and life and to start to feel empowered when it comes to being the CEO of your dance studio.

As one of my mentors Terry Hawkins says, 'There are two times in life, now and too late,' and I hope you take advantage of the now. Turn the page, and let's get started on transforming your dance studio!

To your studio's success!

Clint
Founder & CEO
Dance Studio Owners Association
www.dancestudioownersassociation.com

GET ACCESS TO YOUR BOOK BONUSES BY HEADING TO

WWW.DANCESTUDIOTRANSFORMATION.COM

SCROLL DOWN AND ENTER YOUR CONTACT DETAILS IN THE 'CLAIM YOUR BONUS' SECTION

Chapter One

YOUR STUDIO'S SUCCESS PLAN

'Doing the best at this moment puts you in the best place for the next moment.' ~ Oprah Winfrey

So often, we get caught up in what success should look like that we forget what our version of success is. When we're on our studio journey, we can get so busy being busy that we lose track of the fact that we are human beings who need to get off the treadmill regularly to reflect, reassess and experience joy.

This chapter was never intended to be a part of this book until I had a conversation with one of our new program members. As I was speaking with her, a light bulb went off in my head. She had been working on her marketing strategy and implementing tactics around bringing in new students, but she was doing a million things, being reactive and she was certainly not reaching her full potential as the captain of her studio ship. Why? She had zero idea of what she *actually* wanted to achieve. She knew that new students were important, but she didn't set any goals around the results she wanted to reach.

In my experience, we tend to do that a lot as studio owners. We go from one thing to the next without questioning our actions and without addressing if what we're doing daily is getting us closer to the businesses and lives that we want… generally, because we don't know what that looks like. We haven't taken the time to create solid business goals and then we wonder why our business isn't thriving.

Without a destination you're going to get lost along the way – that's inevitable. You'll waste precious time and lose money, then stress and frustration will usually creep in too! Right now, what are you going for in your studio? Can you look up from this book, gaze over at the wall and see your business goals for the next 90 days clearly laid out in front of you? Do you wake up each morning to a calendar that is blocked out in chunks of time where you'll be ticking tasks off the list that are going to move you closer to achieving those goals?

My aim right now is not to make you feel like an underachiever, or that you're not made for being a business owner. That's totally not the case! My aim is to shine a light on the opportunity you have in front of you and for us, together, to start setting those goals that are going to bring you closer to becoming the 'go to' studio in your area while ensuring you live a life that ROCKS (as my friend and mentor Christina Guidotti would say)!

The other super cool thing about setting goals is that it provides you with clarity, which in turn equals power. When you know where you're headed, the only thing that can stop you moving forward is you. And once you start putting the wheels in motion towards those goals, nothing will be able to stop you. Momentum is powerful – you'll look back in 12 months' time and think 'Wow, look at everything my team and I achieved. Look at how many more lives we're impacting at our studio. I've never felt more alive and happy than I do now.'

Can I let you in on a little secret though? I never thought of myself as a goal setter, but that all changed a year into owning my dance studio with a friend. And while I first heard about goals from my mother when I was about 10 years old, it didn't register completely until I was a little older.

My mother is the person I'm most grateful for in my life, always has been and always will be, and she is the reason you have this book in your hands. She was a single mother, who brought me up on her own in a country town called Camden, west of Sydney, Australia (no, kangaroos do not jump up and down the main streets!). She worked her butt off to give me everything I could have ever wanted. I still remember the day I got home from school after being bullied (I had learning difficulties and all I wanted to do was sing and dance – hello, target for bullying!) and she said to me, 'Clint, there's only one thing

I want for you in your life and that's for you to be happy.' I still get tears in my eyes when I recall this story because this was the moment I decided that I would strive to be happy each and every day of my time on this planet. I knew from an early age that I wanted to design my own life and I'm thrilled to say that I'm now living a life designed by me and only me.

I started dancing at the age of nine, first in jazz and then moving onto tap, ballet and hip hop. In an unexpected turn of events, I started my first dance studio when I was 16 because my old teacher had sold her studio. At the time, parents came to me asking if I could teach their children, as I'd been a student teacher from the age of 14. A dance friend and I decided to give it a go, and in a tiny community hall with 30 students, our small studio was born. This was my first taste of running a business and even with only a small amount of students, I had no idea what I was getting myself into.

I loved dancing and teaching dancing, so of course it made sense to me to open a dance studio. But at that point, I didn't realize how different teaching dance was to actually running a business based around that. In Michael Gerber's book *The E-Myth Revisited*, he talks about moving from being a technician, which is what you are as a dance teacher, to growing and becoming the entrepreneur, which is what you need to do to become a studio owner with a thriving business.

After making a truck load of mistakes those first few years that cost hours and hours of time, late nights, breakdowns (yep, a few bathroom floor moments) and money, I finally saw a light at the end of the tunnel after a conversation with the person who went on to become my first business mentor. That conversation, and the time I spent with this person learning and embracing what it took to run a business, completely changed my life. This is also when the 'Goals' conversation came back up.

She said, 'Clint, no wonder you're exhausted, have no money in the bank and aren't getting the student numbers you need – you haven't spent any time working out what you actually want. You're just getting up each day, doing the same thing and expecting a different result!' Hello, cold, hard but necessary honesty! This wake-up call was exactly what I needed, and in that moment I felt like a weight had been lifted off my shoulders. I felt lighter just knowing that I had someone to help me forge a successful path forward. The first step was creating a vision, on paper, of what I wanted to achieve in my studio then work backwards, creating the strategies and implementing the tactics (steps) that would get me there.

Fast-forward five years and our studio was operating six days a week, with a few hundred students and our classes at capacity. We had built a booming business and I was still only 21. Despite its success, I decided to sell my half of the studio to my business partner and soon after started working at the top celebrity agency in Australia, managing some of the biggest names in television and media.

And boy, did dealing with the dance moms back when I had the studio help when I was dealing with high profile celebrities! Over the five years I was there I was responsible for pitching ideas and securing commercial endorsements, licensing, publishing, television, radio and speaking deals for my stable of high-profile clients.

I remember so clearly the day one of my clients rang me up and said, 'Clint, what new work have you got for me this week? I have this new house and a higher mortgage payment I need to pay.' This sort of call wasn't uncommon, but what I realized in that moment is that we had been working with each other for six months and had not set any goals of what we both wanted during our time working together. 'Aha', I thought as the notion of goals entered my life once again.

During my time at the agency I also created DanceLife, Australia's largest online community for dancers and performers. Over the four years I ran it, DanceLife became Australia's 'go to' destination for all things dance, an online resource for dancers, a large national dance competition (so I fully understand the competition space) and a learn to dance program that was placed in schools throughout the country.

I was really on a roll when it came to setting and achieving goals in this business, hence why I was able to start, scale and sell it within four years. I don't mention this to impress you - I tell you to impress upon you how powerful goal setting can be when it comes to building the 'go to' studio you know you can have.

After selling DanceLife and leaving the agency, I moved on to a role as the Company Manager for the Tony Award winning musical *Jersey Boys*, a role that saw me travelling internationally and managing a team of 56 people.

At the start I was excited as I thought I had just landed my dream job, but I quickly realized that this position wasn't aligned to my values or life goals. So at the end of my contract, I decided to take some time to really work out what I wanted for my life and my career. I'd been go, go, go since I started the studio at 16, and I needed time to reflect, assess and to start the next chapter of my life – living with purpose and with passion. Unfortunately, you can't achieve this in a day!

During my break, I had a call from a dance studio owner who heard I was back in the country. She wanted my help – she was working a crazy amount of hours each week, never seeing her husband or children, felt like she couldn't give her parents and students any more, and to top it off, her bank balance was emptying faster than she could believe.

She asked if I would help her and her studio get back on track. To be honest, I was bored trying to figure out what to do next with my life and I knew dance like the back of my hand, so my answer was, 'Sure, let's do it!'

Since saying those four words, my life has never been the same.

I enjoyed working with her so much that I started to work with more and more studio owners, then offering three-month coaching programs. Only a few years ago, I started setting goals around how I wanted this business to help studio owners around the globe and I'm thrilled to say we're doing it through our online program Studio Success Formula, the Dance Studio Owners Association, our live events plus my 12-month intensive coaching program Dance Studio Owners Inner Circle.

Why have I shared my journey with you? A few reasons. Firstly, so that you know there is no straight line to success and that where you are right now in your business and life is where you're meant to be – trust that. Secondly, without learning the process of setting goals, I may be sitting at a desk job that I hate, working with annoying people who eat their lunch loudly and having a partner that sits on the lounge and plays video games all day (note: that's just my version of a not satisfying life, but yours may be different!).

I think it's time for you and I to map out your studio's success plan for the next 12 months. But before we jump in, this is not a five-minute exercise you do while you're talking on the phone, picking up the groceries from the supermarket or helping your child with their homework.

Look at your diary and block out 60 minutes over the next 48 hours to commit to going through and setting your goals. Warning: by the end of this book, you'll get pretty tired of hearing me say commit and commitment, but it's no accident that I mention these words so often. I mention this because I know that when you commit to something – to change, to transformation, to growing as a leader – that is when your life and studio will start to grow, that's when you'll start to feel more joy and it's also when you'll start to create more freedom in your life. *Snaps* for commitment!

Are you ready to start moving closer to having your dream studio and life? Yes? Then let's jump in!

YOUR DREAM MORNING

It's no surprise that the most successful people in business and life have morning routines; something we've discussed at length inside the Dance Studio Owner's Association. The way you start each morning sets you up to either succeed or just survive your day.

So, how does your ideal day start? What could you do each morning to ensure you are firing on all cylinders during the day? Here's a hint – checking Facebook while you're still in bed isn't one of those things. How could you awaken your body, mind and soul? Would you wake up at your beach home by the water with the most amazing and supportive partner?

Remember, I'm all about helping you design the life you want to live and this is the first step.

Put pen to paper and write out exactly what your dream morning looks and feels like. Don't get in the trap of saying, 'I have children so I can't have that' or 'I'll never be able to afford living near the beach.' This is your life. No excuses... so start design!

From the moment I open my eyes, this is how my ideal morning unfolds...

____

____

____

____

____

How did you go? Every 90 days, my morning routine changes – I like to mix it up and try new things, but meditation, gratitude and exercise are all consistent parts of my routine. I then throw things in like journaling, affirmations and reading to spice things up. My ideal morning always starts with me waking up to the sounds of the waves at the beach, with my loved one throwing their arms around me and saying 'Good morning beautiful!' Choose your own adventure, right?!

My favorite book on morning routines that create success is by my buddy Hal Elrod, who I interviewed for one of our association masterclasses, called *The Miracle Morning*. Make sure you grab a copy, because seriously, simply creating a morning routine can change your life. It did for me and has done the same for many of our studio owners.

YOUR ROLE IN THE STUDIO

Too often, when I first start working with studio owners, I quickly work out that they are underpaid, underappreciated and rarely get time to work on projects and tasks that excite them.

As a studio owner, I know that you're highly creative, but I also know that you want to be making more money for those many hours you're putting into the business and your students, teachers and parents.

So, how can you be the studio owner doing the things that light you up without getting bogged down in low-value tasks like invoicing, sending out newsletters or making changes on the website? Great question – and the first place to start is by writing your own job description. Or as I call it, your 'dream day plan'.

Similar to what you did just a moment ago with your dream morning, I now want you to brain dump all the things you'd love to do during your dream day that contribute to growing your studio – that will also fulfill you creatively.

As the studio owner, my dream day looks like this...

____

____

____

____

____

____

____

____

____

____

There are a couple of things surely running through your mind right now…

1. I'm doing none of the things I wrote down because I'm too busy keeping the studio running.
2. I'm doing some of this now but certainly not enough, so I need to delegate more.
3. Yay, I'm living my dream and have built the best studio I can (if this is you, you don't need this book!)

I get it. You're looking at what you wrote down and you're probably asking yourself, 'Clint, I can't see the path to getting here from where I am now.' Breathe, this is totally normal and the great news is that what I'm walking you through in this book is what's going to get you there. Will it take hard work? Yes. Will it be worth it? ABSOLUTELY!

YOUR STUDIO – YOUR VALUES

Gone are the days when your studio is the only option for your potential parents and students. While I'll be giving you my branding formula to make you stand out from the pack in Chapter 6 (Building Your Locally Famous Brand), the first thing you need to get clear on are your values.

You can go to http://www.value-test.com/ValueTest1.php to take part in a free test that will have you answering a number of questions that will give you a list of your values in order of priority. You can do this for your business as well as for you personally, if you like.

Knowing your values will be the foundation to build a solid brand that allows you to position your studio as a business like no other in the area. Once you have gone through the test, list your business values below.

What Are The Top 7 Values For Your Studio?

1. ______________________________

2. ______________________________

3. ______________________________

4. ______________________________

5. ______________________________

6. ______________________________

7. ______________________________

WHAT ARE YOUR CUSTOMERS SAYING ABOUT YOU?

It makes me laugh when studio owners rack their brain for hours trying to come up with what makes their studio different. Maybe you've asked yourself questions like: 'Why do people come to us?', 'What makes us unique?', 'How can we be different so we don't look like every other dance studio?'

The truth is, you just need to look within your studio to find these answers. Go to your current students and parents and start by asking two questions (this is great in a survey):

1. Why did you join our studio?
2. Why do you stay at our studio?

These questions are so powerful and will assist you greatly when creating your brand and marketing plan that actually attracts your ideal parents and students.

What did they say? Write down 10 words or phrases that your customers used to describe your studio:

1. ______________________________

2. ______________________________

3. ______________________________

4. ______________________________

5. ______________________________

6. ______________________________

7. ______________________________

8. ______________________________

9. ______________________________

10. ______________________________

WHERE DO YOU WANT TO BE?

Every studio owner has a gap between where they are and where they want to be in their business. It's crucial that you're aware of exactly where your studio is right now and the goals you have in place over the next three, six and twelve months.

Now, you won't need to share this with anyone, but it's time to get real on some of the numbers in your business. More importantly, I want you to dream big about where you want to be if you achieve all of your three, six and twelve month goals.

My only instruction when filling this out is to be honest with yourself when it comes to creating your goals.

Student Numbers

Today I have ________ students and ________ families.
In three months I have ________ students and ________ families.
In six months I have ________ students and ________ families.
In twelve months I have ________ students and ________ families.

Class Capacities

Today my classes are at ____% full (work out your average class capacity across your classes).
In three months my classes are at ____% full.
In six months my classes are at ____% full.
In 12 months my classes are at ____% full.

Wage

Today I'm taking a wage of ________________ per month.
In three months I'm taking a wage of ________________ per month.
In six months I'm taking a wage of ________________ per month.
In 12 months I'm taking a wage of ________________ per month.

Revenue

Today my studio is making __________ per month in net profit (after tax and expenses).
In three months my studio is making __________ per month in net profit.
In six months my studio is making __________ per month in net profit.
In 12 months my studio is making __________ per month in net profit.

Teaching Hours

(As a studio owner you want to reduce your teaching hours to work on bigger income generating projects and promotions)
Today I'm teaching ______ hours per week.
In three months I'm teaching ______ hours per week.
In six months I'm teaching ______ hours per week.
In 12 months I'm teaching ______ hours per week.

Working Hours

Today I'm working in the studio ______ hours per week.
In three months I'm working in the studio ______ hours per week.
In six months I'm working in the studio ______ hours per week.
In 12 months I'm working in the studio ______ hours per week.

Free Time

Today I'm spending ______ hours per week doing the things I love that have nothing to do with the business (reading, spending time with family, day trips, picnics, shopping, sleeping in, etc.).
In three months I'm spending ______ hours per week doing the things I love that have nothing to do with the business.
In six months I'm spending ______ hours per week doing the things I love that have nothing to do with the business.
In 12 months I'm spending ______ hours per week doing the things I love that have nothing to do with the business.

Vacation/Holidays

In the last three months I've had ______ weeks off from the business.
In the next three months I've had ______ weeks off from the business.
In the next six months I've had ______ weeks off from the business.
In the next 12 months I've had ______ weeks off from the business.

How do you feel? Straight up, I'm going to let you know that if you've shed a tear or feel disappointed that you're not further ahead, you're not alone. Wipe those tears because the most important thing you need to take away and focus on from the above is the opportunity that lies before you: the chance to finally build the business and life you have always wanted.

Now What?

Now that you have these goals in front of you, you can see where you want to go and the next step is for us to start creating an action plan to get you at each milestone: three months, six months and twelve months. This book is going to give you the step by step strategies and tactics to ensure you move closer and closer to those goals.

SEE IT, DO IT, ACHIEVE IT!

It's important that what you have just written down on paper and committed to goes up on the wall or in a place that you see multiple times during the day. Maybe it becomes the wallpaper on your phone or you print it out on a big piece of paper that you look at every morning before you start your day. Mine sits above my laptop so during the day when I look up, I ask myself, 'Is what I'm working on now contributing to getting me closer to these goals?'

Your future, the future of your studio, is in your hands, as is the resource that is going to hold your hand during the journey ahead.

I'm here for you. Now you know what you want and where you're going, let's dive into your business and start making some sustainable changes to bring you more impact, income and inspiration.

Chapter Two

KNOWING YOUR NUMBERS

'A year from now you may wish
you had started today.' ~ Karen Lamb

I still remember the day I finally finished creating our money box for fees in woodwork class. I'd been working on this box, where the lid slides on and off, so parents could place their fees in an envelope with the cash inside and we could just pop it in the box. I'd then go home after each night and reconcile the payments with what was in the spreadsheet. Hello, manual labor!

Today, times have changed. We can do everything online. We have studio software and cloud based accounting systems. We have apps for our tablets and smartphones, and we can set up all our customers on direct debit systems so all we need to do is push a button and money gets popped into our bank account. These days, there is so much more to keep us on track when it comes to the finances in our business.

With new ways of doing things and more options, it has created confusion for studio owners globally around what works and what numbers you really need to know to grow your business without needing to be an accountant – and without it sucking up all your time.

This chapter is about you getting comfortable with the important numbers in your business. Don't worry, I never enjoyed knowing or looking at any of the numbers in my studio until I found someone who could break it down, tell me exactly what to focus on and how to interpret them in a way that would help me grow the business and deal quickly with any red flags. And that's exactly what I'm going to give you here.

FINANCIAL FRIDAYS

I'm going to share with you one of the best things we implemented into our studio – in fact, every other business I have created and sold – and that's Financial Fridays. For 60 minutes each Friday morning, I go through all the important figures in the business. And when I say figures, I'm not just talking about money in and money out – I'm talking about being across where all your numbers are at including new student enrollments, drop outs and so on. Right now I want you to open your diary and block out the same 60 minutes every Friday for you and the numbers to get familiar with each other. Don't break this commitment for anything; it's an important one and as we walk through this chapter, you'll understand why!

Stay With Me – I want you to make me a promise – that you'll stay with me during these next two chapters where we'll dig into all things money and finances. As an industry, we need to be able to talk more openly about money. Just like the local hairdresser, beautician or mechanic, we are providing a highly valuable service that needs to be paid for. Do you have fear or guilt around money or think that running your studio out of pure passion is enough? It's not. You will only last so long on the passion journey before you end up working 70 hours a week, earning no money… and that passion will quickly fade, replaced with a bitter, angry studio owner. My aim is to stop this happening!

Remember, it's you who is changing the lives of your students every day. As we all know, dance classes are so much more than just dance classes; they provide you with life skills to become the best version of yourself. You deserve to be paid for that.

IF YOU FAIL TO PLAN, YOU PLAN TO FAIL

Two staple documents that every studio owner needs to have in place: a one-page list of projected expenses and income for that dance season. You can probably tell that these documents will complement the goals you completed in Chapter 1, but this is where we put our money where our mouth is. As an aside, if you're reading this and you're halfway into the season no problem, do it for the rest of the season – no excuses, okay?

If you have the data available, a great place to start is by looking back over the last two years and reviewing your income and expenses. If you're a new studio owner you have the opportunity to jump in with both feet and create the figures you want (you'll want to do a little research first).

Once you have the numbers in place, it's time to sit with your goals and figures from the previous years and work out where you want to be financially in terms of income, expenses and profit for the next 12 months.

I still do this each year, and I absolutely love it. I dedicate a few hours a day in the morning across a week to come up with my financial plan and targets that scare me, yet don't seem unrealistic, because there's a fine line.

When it comes to holding all business-related documents, I'm a Google Drive fan and suggest you set up your free account there as well. Once you've done that, you can set up a simple Google Sheet, where all your numbers can live.

For the projected expenses that are relevant for your studio, you'll need to look at a wide range of things:

Accountants bills, bathroom items, books, courses, training, cleaners, client drinks and food, costumes, event venue hire, external venue hire (concert), furniture, gifts (staff and students), insurance, internet, marketing – general, marketing – live events, marketing – online, marketing – partners, marketing – print, merchandise, mobile phone, music royalties, overseas travel – air/accom, rent/studio, hire/repayments, shop – snack and drinks, staff wages – office staff, staff wages – owner/s, staff wages – teachers, stationery, studio equipment – mirrors, sound system, studio phone, studio, repairs/renovations, subscriptions (online software), uniform, utilities – gas, water and electricity, virtual assistant, website costs etc.

Every studio is different, but you'll be able to see from previous years where your money is going and put in some solid estimates. Make sure you break it up into daily, weekly, monthly and yearly expenses so you can really see what you're working with.

GETTING SAVVY WITH YOUR EXPENSES

For dance studio owners, I know the margins can be very slim, particularly if you have high rent and a big team. I want to share with you four simple ways to reduce business expenses. None of these are necessarily 'secrets', but simply things that many studio owners either don't know or forget to do. When done correctly, any one of these items will reduce your expenses significantly and allow you to sleep better at night knowing that you have a solid grip on your business.

But before I give you these tips, I want you to know that not all expenses are bad. On the contrary, many expenses we pay out in our business actually allow us to grow it. Ideally, you want to drive up profits in your studio and to do that you may need to dish out some more cash, into the right areas of course – like marketing, but more on that soon.

So, the four 'secrets'...

1. Reduce utility costs – The first step to reducing utility costs is to look closely at what items you are paying for. For example, telephone rates have been dropping for years. If you have had the same plan for more than a year, you should revisit it and look at areas for potential savings. It's worth looking at your cell phone bill, insurance bills, office telephone bill, and even your electricity bill. For your electricity, you might not have a choice of providers, but you can look at using appliances and lighting that are designed to save energy.

2. Always ask for a discount – From toilet supplies to your internet service, frequently discounts are available for many of the items that you purchase – you just need to ask. You can often receive a discount for signing a contract or purchasing an additional needed service, but if you don't ask, you don't get!

3. Cut out paper – In this day and age, almost everything that you need to do for your office and marketing can be done digitally. It's oh-so-easy to maintain all of your records online, use email to communicate, and do much of your marketing and advertising online. Not only are you helping the environment, but you're reducing expenses and giving yourself access to all of your information from anywhere.

4. Barter, every chance you get – Look for opportunities to barter as often as possible. It's likely that you work with businesses that could use your services, so you can barter those services for theirs. For example, if you need a caterer for an open day/house, you might have a student whose parent is a professional caterer – you may be able to barter studio tuition for food at your event.

INCOME INSIDE THE STUDIO

Once you have projected those expenses it's time to look at your income; the revenue that is flowing into the studio. In Chapter 3, I'll dive into the different revenue streams that exist in a dance studio, but for now let's identify where you may be generating income from: birthday parties, costumes, exams, group lessons, merchandise, private lessons, recital/concert, shop – snacks and drinks, studio hire, sponsorship, uniforms, workshops, VIP program etc.

Remember, what we are doing on this first step is projecting what we want to achieve financially with our studio over the next 12 months. As a reminder, have your goals from Chapter 1 next to you when you do this so you have consistency and clarity on where you are headed.

Once you have sat down and worked out your projected expenses and income for the year, you'll have a clearer understanding of the expected profit that you will generate, which you can then allocate to further education, big ticket studio purchases, staff etc. We might think, 'Ugh, numbers'... but this is a really exciting task to do! Picture it now – seeing exactly where you want to head financially with your studio on one page that you can revisit daily. Do yourself a favor and don't skip this important step, otherwise everything else you learn in this book won't make as much impact as it could.

I am no accountant, but one of the best things I did early on in my business was seek out the best financial advisors. Every studio owner should have an accountant who they can work with on finances and taxes for their business.

Once you've done the above exercise around your projected figures, organize a time to meet with your accountant to go through it, ask for their advice and, most importantly, have them hold you accountable to your goals.

FUN FINANCIAL REPORTS TO FOCUS ON

Each week in your studio on Financial Fridays, I'm encouraging you to focus on just three reports:

1. Profit & Loss Statement
2. Balance Sheet
3. Weekly Report

Each of these reports will show you exactly where you're at in your studio, highlight any problem areas and allow you to really understand what's going on financially in the business. No matter what staff you have supporting you in your business, it's crucial for you, the studio owner, to be across all aspects of how the business is performing financially.

Back when I started running the studio and my mentor told me that I needed to have a more intimate relationship with the numbers in the studio, I was not impressed. In fact, I was highly resistant! It took me about six weeks to get on board but as soon as I did, our business started to grow – and I started to fall in love with the numbers. I'm hoping it doesn't take you six weeks, but I can assure you that once you start to pay attention and look at these three reports, the way you view and operate your studio will change for the better.

Let's walk through these three reports now…

Profit & Loss Statement (Income Statement)

This statement shows you a summary of the income and expenses for your studio. The profit and loss statement will inform you whether your business made or lost money for the week/month that you're reviewing. It's calculated first by entering your revenue, known as the top line, and then subtracts the costs of doing business, including cost of goods sold, operating expenses, tax expense and interest expense. What's left is your bottom line, which is the net income, also known as your profit.

Balance Sheet

A balance sheet is a snapshot of what your studio owns (assets) and owes (liabilities) at the time of running the report (weekly or monthly).

Your balance sheet is split into three areas:

- Assets – including cash, equipment (barres, mirrors, laptops), goodwill, money owed to business, stock
- Liabilities – including credit card debts, loans, money owed to suppliers and tax liabilities
- Owner's equity – the amount left after liabilities are deducted from assets

Weekly Report

Your profit and loss statement and your balance sheet are generic financial reports that every business needs to generate, but the weekly report is something I created just for my dance studio owner clients. It gives you a glimpse at how your business is performing in all its key areas and compares your results this week to last week, and month to month. Again, you can create your report in a Google Sheet, which means you can have your team edit the document so that everyone knows how you're tracking.

Your weekly report should include the following statistics; make sure you track them every single week. Consistency is KEY!

FINANCES
Fees Paid
Fees Outstanding
Other Income Paid
Other Income Outstanding
Staff Wages Paid
Other Expenses Paid

STUDENTS
Current Student Numbers
Current Total Families
Attendance %

New Student Enquiries
New Students Came In
New Student Enquiry Enrollments
Conversion Rate %
Student Drop-Offs
Exit Surveys Sent
Percentage Drop-Off %

CUSTOMER SERVICE
Concerns & Complaints Received
Solutions Provided
Feedback Forms Received
Testimonials Received

TEACHERS
Current Teacher Numbers
Feedback Forms Received

MARKETING
Database Numbers
New Facebook Likes
Total Facebook Likes
Total Facebook Posts
New Instagram Followers
Total Instagram Followers
Total Instagram Posts

THE TOOLS YOU NEED

When it comes to getting a clear picture of where you're at financially in your business, it's best to have a studio software system in place – for example, Jack Rabbit, DanceBiz or Studio Director, plus have an accounting cloud-based software program such as Xero or Quickbooks. Your accountant will be able to assist you with these or contact the service provider who will be more than helpful. I know studio owners who have worked with all the suppliers above, and love them and the customer service they provide.

ULTIMATE PROFIT PLAN

Now that you know where you want your studio to head over the next 12 months, and you know the numbers you need to be looking at each week in your business, I want us to take a closer look at your classes. We're going to look at your class sizes, how profitable your classes are, patterns across age groups, styles and class types to determine opportunities. Growing current class numbers through enrolling more new students and increasing the average number of classes each child takes is key to boosting the profit in your studio.

WHERE IS YOUR MONEY COMING FROM?

Right now, what is your most profitable class? How about your most profitable dance style? Do you know your most profitable age group? If you don't know these off the top of your head, that's okay because you will – and once you apply what I'm teaching you in this book, you'll be unstoppable!

The reason I want you to know this information? If you can say to me, 'Clint, my 3-4 year olds are my most profitable group and within that, fairy ballet is the most popular style. Therefore, it brings me the most amount of profit,' we can use this information to plan and execute a solid marketing campaign directly to your ideal parent avatar. And in turn, this will generate more new student leads for those classes, or for you to open up more classes for that age group and style.

By knowing these numbers, you could also tell me which of your classes is the least profitable. Now, there are multiple reasons for underperforming classes, including the teacher, the area you're in, class time and day that it runs. It's amazing how many studio owners I start working with and ask to work out their class capacities, only for them to realize that they have a handful of classes operating in the red that they never knew were costing them money. Better to find out now than never, I say!

CLARITY ON CLASS CAPACITIES

I'm now going to run you through the formula for calculating how each of your classes are performing within your studio, but most importantly the opportunity that sits in front of you to increase your numbers and grow your business. That's the fun stuff right there!

Put the following details into a Google Sheet to make calculating the numbers a breeze.

1. Class name

2. Age group of class

3. Style of dance

4. Teacher of the class

5. Current number of students in the class
This is the number of students you currently have in that class.

6. Price per class
This is the price that each child pays for that class. Depending on your pricing model, you may need to calculate the average price of the classes if you have a sliding scale fee structure or capped class model, or you can work them out individually to get a true figure.

7. Current income for class
How much income does the class make you currently, with the current student numbers?

8. Current expenses to run class
How much does this class cost you to run including the teacher's wage?

9. Potential maximum student numbers in class
How many students could you fit in this class?

10. Potential maximum income for class
If your class was at full capacity (the number above), how much income would you be making?

11. Potential maximum expenses for class
If you had the class operating at maximum capacity, how much would

expenses be? This may be the same as your current expenses if you don't want or have to put on an additional teacher to cope with more students.

12. Current class capacity
To work out how full you are currently, you want to take your current student numbers and divide it by your potential maximum numbers. Then times it by 100 to get the percentage of how full your class is now.

13. Difference in income result
This will tell you how much more income you could be making per week if you reached full capacity, not including any additional expenses (full class income minus current class income)

14. Difference in expenses result
This will tell you the additional expenses you would incur weekly if you reached full capacity (full class expenses minus current class expenses)

15. Potential additional income each week
This is my favorite number. This will give you your profit for that one class for the week if you reach your full capacity. Simply take the number from step 13 and minus step 14 and you will end up with your profit – the magic word!

Let me give you an example of how this could look for your studio:

Let's pretend that I'm filling out my Google Sheet starting with step one in the formula. In class name I have Groovy Groovers, it's for six-year-olds and the style is jazz, Mr Clint takes the class, there are currently 15 students in this class each paying $15 per class, hence my income is $225 per class. My current expenses to run this class after I take out teacher, venue, bills etc (simply look at your weekly expenses and divide it by the number of classes you have and you'll get your average class expense). I end up with $80 for expenses. I have added 20 as the maximum students I could take in that class, which will automatically give me $300 as the class income and the expense stays the same at $80, as I don't need an additional teacher. My class is currently 75% full, if I have 20 students in the class then my additional income would be $75 per week and additional expenses is $0, leaving me with a profit of $75 per week for that one class. Over a 42-week dance year, that's an additional $3,150 for getting just five new students into just one of my classes.

When you complete this step for each class you offer, you're going to really see the growth potential for your studio. It's an exciting thing to see on screen or on paper what opportunities lie ahead for your business!

This process will take time, but it's part of building your solid business foundation for the studio. You will collect so much amazing data by completing this sheet – you will be able to see those age groups that are most and least profitable, those teachers who run the most and least profitable classes, the dance styles that are most and least popular, plus loads more. So many studio owners have had many 'Aha!' moments after completing this exercise, so what are you waiting for?

PERFECT CLASS PRICING

There are hundreds of pricing models a dance studio can implement, from the flat fee to the tiered to the made-up pricing model. I'm going to walk you through two pricing models that have worked for our program members, and also share with you some strategies on discounts and payment methods.

When jumping into pricing their classes and additional services, many studio owners have come up with their prices based on what the studio up or down the road has done. This is a mistake. Sure, you need to be aware of what your competitors are offering and charging, but the one big secret I'd love to share with you right away is that people don't come to your studio because of the price – they come because of the way you make them feel during and outside of the classroom. But more on that later!

You may be sick of hearing about the numbers in your business right now, but as I mentioned straight up, it's the key to whether your studio sinks or swims. Although we are only into Chapter 2 of the book, you may be feeling a little overwhelmed and that's okay – in fact, it's required, because growth does not sit in comfort. There's no magic switch to make change happen in your studio, but that's why you have this book and me – to ensure you get the results you want by taking the right type of action that I describe in Dance Studio Transformation.

Let me take you through the two main pricing models I see working inside successful dance studios:

Flat Fee Pricing Structure

Flat fee pricing structure for your group classes isn't as popular as it should be. I see many studio owners who have successfully implemented this pricing model, which is simple and works.

Now, there are multiple variations of a flat fee pricing structure and this is dependent on whether you decide to create the prices based on age group, class duration or level. Let's look at a few examples.

Shake It Up Studios – Flat Fee Structure

They are based on class duration only.
30 minute class is $10.00
45 minute class is $12.50
1 hour class is $15.00
1.5 hour class is $18.00

They have this pricing model for all ages, across all styles and all streams (your studio may have a fun stream and a performance stream).

Shuffle Dance Studio – Flat Fee Structure

They base their fees on duration and stream.

Fun Stream
30 minute class is $11.00
45 minute class is $12.00
1 hour class is $14.00

Performance Stream (perform at competitions etc)
45 minute class is $15.00
1 hour class is $17.00
1.5 hour class is $19.00

With the flat fee structure, you can also base the price on the age. If you're looking at implementing a flat fee structure, my advice is to do it via duration, to keep things consistent across the board. Plus, it's more effective during the point of invoicing and parents will not get confused and bombard you with emails and phone calls!

Tiered Pricing Model

Tiered pricing models are very popular as the train of thought is that it encourages students to take more classes. Remember though that people are buying the experience, so while it may help get them in the door to a new class, there are many other economical ways we can make this happen without discounting.

In saying that, I've seen a tiered pricing structure work extremely well. My main concern with a tiered model is that it can get messy on your admin side and the parents can get a little confused. So, if you have to use a tiered structure, ensure you have really clear communication laid out to explain it.

When creating a sliding scale for your classes it can get complicated when you have classes with multiple durations. As an example, Lizzy is 13 and she attends classes in ballet, tap and jazz. Her ballet class is one hour and tap and jazz are both 45 minutes. She's effectively doing three classes, but one of those classes is longer in duration.

I'm going to show you a tiered model that we've implemented with studio owners who wanted to stick with a sliding scale.

One important thing to note that helps make a sliding scale fee structure manageable and successful is to only offer two durations of classes (45 and 60 minutes are good).

Jazz Hands Dance Studio

1 x Class $16.00
2 x Classes $30.00 (-$2)
3 x Classes $44 (-4$)
4 x Classes $58 (-$6)
5 x Classes $72 (-$8)
6 x Classes $86 (-$10)
7 x Classes + $100 (-$12)

This model is about discounting on the total price of the total amount of classes. As an example, if they were to do four classes at $16 it would cost $64. What we've done here is discount the class by an additional

$2 each additional class. Stay with me here! You can see here that four classes is discounted by $6.

There are also hybrid versions of these pricing models. Some studios have a sliding scale for all their fun classes, but a flat fee for performance classes.

DODGE THE DISCOUNTS

Now let's talk about a word that's not one of my favorites... Discounting. I'm a big believer that unless you're in a product-based business that relies on you selling massive volumes of products (like soap), then you don't discount. Owning a dance studio means you're in the service industry. By discounting the services, some people may view your training as not of the same quality as the studio down the road. For me, it's about delivering the best training and customer service possible and therefore people should pay the fee for it.

In saying that, I wanted to give you some examples of discounts many studio owners have implemented over the years. I stand pretty firm on my no-discounting policy, but wanted to share these with you.

Multiple Class Discount

You may have a flat fee pricing model but can incorporate a percentage off if they attend four or more classes as an example. In terms of the discount it can range between 5-10%.

Family Discount

To encourage family members to come along to class you could offer a 5-10% discount off their fees to the family members that enroll in dance classes.

Early Bird Payment

Some studios have trouble getting in payments on time therefore introduce an early bird discount, i.e. If you pay within the first two days of the month, you receive a 5-10% discount.

Unlimited Class Pass

This can apply for either pricing models. Once students hit a certain amount of classes each week, then they don't need to pay for any additional classes. Be careful with this one though, as I once worked with a studio owner who had an unlimited class option and it worked out that they were earning about $2.50 per class. Not ideal.

Before you discount, I'd like you to work out your class fee income for the entire year without the discount, then with the discount. Now compare the two. I'm certainly not about being greedy, so what I suggest to studio owners is to then allocate 60-80% of the difference to a WOW Fund. This WOW fund is to be used throughout the year to bring in some guest teachers, run a studio picnic or take your students out of town for an external workshop. I can tell you now that this will make a much greater impact on your studio in terms of retention, referrals and recommendations than a discount.

HOW TO GET FEES IN THE DOOR

I know asking for money and overdue fees isn't the most thrilling thing to talk about, and I get that it's a tough conversation to have. But let's get one thing straight here – you are running a business, not a charity. You may call this tough love, but it's like a jab in the heart every time a studio owner comes to me asking for help, as there's a chance that their parents and staff are walking all over them. A word of guidance – you are not here to make sure everyone else is okay, you're here to provide the most amazing training and experiences for your students and parents. But to do this, you need to be making money, and that money needs to come in on time!

Direct Debit – There is no reason why any dance studio should not be using or starting to use a direct debit system in their studio. Gone are days of invoicing each month and chasing money – nearly every other industry including karate, swim school and gymnastics uses the direct debit system. I've seen those studio owners who make the switch free up so much admin time for them or their staff, they know when money is coming in and overall it makes for a smoother operation.

WRAPPING UP THE NUMBERS

We have covered a lot in Chapter 2, and your brain may be hurting a little (sorry!). But in all honesty, it needs to feel a little strained or you wouldn't be learning anything new. There's been a lot of information to process, so I suggest you re-read this chapter again over the next couple of days to allow it to sink in. Once it does, start putting those financial systems and reports in place – this is the first part of stepping into the CEO of the studio that you know you can be!

Chapter Three

ADDITIONAL REVENUE STREAMS FOR PROFIT

'Don't put all your eggs in one basket.' ~ Warren Buffett

A danger that I see with many studio owners just like you from across the globe is the lack of ways you are generating revenue inside your business. Most of you reading this book will generate the majority of your revenue from group classes and that's smart, but there are additional ways for you to increase the income coming into your studio without having to bring more new students through the door.

Think about how many students you have in your studio currently – they are already in the door, they love your studio and they are the first people who will buy something else from you that is of value to them.

Too often we focus on new students, new students, new students, to boost our bottom line. And while enrolling new students each week is important for the growth of the business, you have a whole bunch of super fans inside your studio each day that are ready to take on a new class, buy a limited edition tank top or sign up to your monthly VIP program.

So when it comes to looking at introducing new revenue streams into your studio, it should be an exciting venture. Yes, it takes work, but you definitely should not put this into the too hard basket as it's going to bring you more income, lift the profits in your studio, and better serve your customers!

I know you will have group classes down pat by now, but later on, I'll be sharing with you a bunch of proven ways to attract new students into your group classes. For this chapter, however, we're going to focus on the additional revenue streams that are a prime opportunity for you to start implementing into your business.

I'm now going to lay out the 11 revenue streams that exist in a dance studio and walk you through how you can get these up and running in your dance studio, moving you even closer to becoming the 'go to' studio in your area!

1. Birthday Parties
2. Costumes
3. Group Lessons (you already know how these work)
4. Limited Edition Merchandise
5. Private Lessons
6. Recital/Concert
7. Shop – Snacks & Drinks
8. Studio Hire
9. Uniforms
10. Workshops & Camps
11. VIP Program

BIRTHDAY PARTIES

The thought of running a birthday party might make you feel a bit queasy (never work with kids or animals, don't they say?), but hear me out for a minute. Some studios don't operate on weekends and if you do, it's generally Saturday, not Sunday. Birthday parties are another great source of additional income, plus it's another great opportunity for your ideal new students to be exposed to your space!

True, it is more work, but it's work you get paid for whether you run them yourself or you simply form a partnership with one or a few local party companies, in which they can hire the space from you, run the parties, clean up and leave. Your job? Take the fee and enjoy your weekend!

Alternatively, you can run the parties in house and have your teachers run the party – it's up to you. I have seen both ways work really well all around the globe. Have a think and make a decision whether you want to create your own party brand or if you want to partner with an existing party business and rent them your space. Whatever you decide, one tip is to ensure every child who attends the party receives some information about your studio along with an exclusive offer for attending the party. You may give them a magnet or flyer or keyring... think of something they and their parents can keep that encourages them to take action (say, make the offer valid for the next seven days only).

While we're on the topic of parties, one useful way to promote your parties is through group buying deals – I'm talking sites like Groupon, Spreets and LivingSocial. You will only make a small amount of profit through these, but think about how many ideal students it could bring through your door. It's then your job to follow them up. More on the student enrollment process in Chapter 7.

COSTUMES

Some studio owners are super clever when it comes to costumes for performances, competitions and recitals/concerts, while some just create more work for themselves while losing money. There are a few ways studio owners manage costumes:

1. Have them created locally or overseas, with parents paying for them outright to keep them.
2. Have them created locally or overseas, with parents hiring them for the performance. The studio will keep the costumes for re-hire in the future.

Both ways can work extremely well, but one thing you need to be above all else is organized if you want your costumes to generate profit for your studio. Costumes and their prices should never come as a shock or surprise to you, your parents and students. I certainly agree with trying to find the best prices for materials, dressmakers and ready to wear items, but you need to also be paid for the time you spend sourcing all of these items and coordinating the entire costume process.

Depending on the size of your studio, it may be you or a costume manager or a staff member working on this project. The biggest mistake that studio owners make when delving into the costume process is giving parents a price before actually working out a budget. This exercise, which could only take you a few hours, will save you plenty of wasted hours down the track – and more importantly, money. Ensure you have all the figures written down, add your margin for the time you and your staff put into the process and then give parents the price.

LIMITED EDITION MERCHANDISE

Limited edition merchandise is an untapped revenue stream that many studios don't take full advantage of. Not only is it great to boost revenue and profit if done correctly, if you select the right items to sell then your students will be wearing your gear everywhere. Hello, free marketing tool!

We're going to talk uniforms in this chapter, but in a nutshell, I'm a big believer in having uniform staple items that don't change. That way, you can add limited edition merchandise pieces into the mix to jazz things up and to increase the revenue you make through merchandise.

Creating Your Limited Range

Firstly, you need to work out what your students would be interested in wearing, by speaking to your existing students or visiting fashion stores to see what's 'in'. The big mistake studio owners make when coming up with merchandise is that they buy what *they* want, but remember, studio owners are not the ideal customer. When you give the customer what they want – read: on-trend fashion items – they will jump at them. Aside from fashion items you can also do products like dance bags and drink bottles. There is a great website called Ali Baba where you can purchase these types of items in bulk at an affordable price – Google it and have a browse around to see what will work for your studio. More about creating an email marketing campaign to sell your limited edition merchandise in Chapter 8.

PRIVATE LESSONS

These are a great way for your teachers to make additional income as well as your business, but the benefits don't stop there. It's also fantastic for retention. In the studios I've worked with, students that have private lessons are more likely to stay longer at a studio than those who don't.

There are two main ways to structure private lessons:

1. The student can pay the teacher directly, you offer this as an additional service for your students and it helps with teacher retention as you're doing them a favor.

2. The student pays you and you take a certain percentage of the fee to cover the cost of rent and utilities and pass on the rest to the teacher.

Another bonus is that private lessons are a great way to use the studio space when it's vacant (white space)!

RECITAL/CONCERT

Your annual recital or concert is an exciting time for everyone! It's also a very busy time of year. There are many expenses associated with running an event such as this, including the venue. Sure, you will make money by selling tickets to the event, but one additional way to generate further income is through sponsorship. Many local business owners would love to get in front of your parents, students, friends and family members. Through logo placement on your website, the show program or in emails promoting the event, you can easily generate further income without too much additional work. Simply create a list of 20 or so local businesses like health clubs, hairdressers, beauty salons, local supermarkets and send them through an email that talks about your concert and the type of people attending who will be their ideal clients. Put together two sponsorship packages that include the ideas I mentioned and charge them a fee. The fee will be dependent on the size of audience you're expecting and the area your studio is located. This is also a great opportunity for you to start creating strategic partnerships with other local businesses where you can help each other's business grow.

SHOP – SNACKS AND DRINKS

Now, having a shop to purchase drinks and some snacks isn't going to buy you that private island you've always wanted, but it will add to the bottom line. Having a fridge with some water, healthy juices and wholesome snacks can definitely give your bank account a bit of a boost. On your busier days and nights in the studio, you may want to bring in some more substantial items for lunch or dinners. This can seem like more work than it's worth and to be honest, it can be. A few of our studio owners may have a parent or parents who run the shop during these busy times who also prepare all the larger meals and take the costs – with the profits either going back to the studio or contributing to the fundraising kitty. The other benefit of offering drinks and food at the studio is that your parents and students will appreciate it.

STUDIO HIRE

If you have your own studio that you either own, rent or lease, then there are probably times when you have free space that you could hire out to external hirers. Many studio owners can increase the use of their free space through external hirers. Think outside the box and create a list of local businesses that could potentially use your studio. Let's create a list together.

- Pilates, yoga, meditation classes
- Community or meet up groups
- Pre schools or local schools for sport

While this is a great opportunity to maximize your revenue, it's also very valuable as many people will be utilizing your space and becoming aware of your business. These people would probably never have known you existed, otherwise!

Depending on what country you live in, you can also advertise your spaces for rent through directory sites including Craigslist and Gumtree. You can also look around your local area including shopping centers and malls that may have notice boards where you can put a poster up for your available venue for hire.

OFFER CLASSES FOR LOCAL BUSINESSES

Something a little bit left of field you may want to think about is offering local businesses dance classes during lunch breaks. This is a great, fun and creative way for teams to bond, not to mention an alternative to competitive team sports. You would charge the company a fee per person, per week on an eight-week course, as an example. Over the eight weeks they could learn just one style or mix it up a bit. Again, this will mean your studio is getting used when it's generally empty, and you'll be getting in moms and dads from your local area who, you guessed it, probably have children or are planning to have children. This is a great example of making money while you market!

Right now I'd love you to make a list of 10 local businesses that ideally have more than 10 staff who you could approach about your corporate dance program. Give it a fun name and push the benefits of team bonding, exercise and fun, and the idea of it being a great alternative to competitive sport. There is stacks of research out there around employees being disengaged and loads of evidence that proves exercise, laughter and taking a break from the desk increases engagement. Put together your case and start developing your corporate lunchtime program! Also remember that you don't need to take the class yourself; this could be great for one of your teachers who is looking for more work.

UNIFORMS

Loads of studio owners I speak with daily have been setting up extremely successful uniform departments in their studios. They have set up a small-designated space to sell retail items from their studio, sometimes in the office area, and sell everything from branded studio uniform items to limited edition merchandise as mentioned earlier. You can also set up an online store to sell your uniforms through Shopify.

When creating your uniform, start with a few key pieces – popular items include tracksuits, singlets, tops and shorts or pants. I want you to survey your students and parents before taking action and getting uniforms made, and once you have that information back and have sourced someone to make the uniforms (local or overseas), announce the uniforms and start getting pre-orders. Use the principle of scarcity and let your studio know that you won't be taking any more uniform orders until a certain date. This will create a 'need it now' mentality for your students and therefore bring in more orders in the one hit, rather than in dribs and drabs. This also means no stock sitting on the floor gathering dust! It's worth keeping a few popular sizes in stock for those new student enrollments.

Having studio uniforms also has many additional benefits aside from increased income including:

- Encouraging discipline
- Helping students resist peer pressure to buy stylish clothes for class
- Helping to identify non-students in the studio
- Diminishing economic and social barriers between students
- Increasing a sense of belonging and school pride
- Improving attendance

WORKSHOPS & CAMPS

Workshops and camps are one of my favorite additional revenue streams on the list. There are plenty of dance studios that run holiday workshops, but right now I want to run through with you the various ways that you can run workshops – and how to make the most from these events financially and ensure you're giving big value to the dancers coming along.

Let's define the different types of workshops and camps, six in total:

Internal Once-Off Teacher Workshop

This is when you run a once off workshop for a couple of hours for your current students with a teacher who is already working with you. You could organize a few teachers to take a number of dance classes back to back and make it a dance class marathon, which you would charge for. To be honest this is not going to be the most profitable, but it certainly helps with retention.

Internal Once-Off Guest Teacher Workshop

Here, you can run a number of different age group and level workshops with a guest teacher. This may be during the holidays or one afternoon when the studio is free. Students pay per class. Although we will discuss retention in upcoming modules, the added benefit of this is the fact that your students will love it and post all about it over social media... which increases your brand awareness and retention of current students.

Multiple Day Internal Teacher Workshop

These are your regular holiday 2-5 day workshops that you run for your existing students. You put on a number of classes daily with your existing teachers for different age groups and levels. During these days you could also provide lunch for the students and include the catering in the cost. Pricing for these multiple days could be a per day cost, then a discounted rate if they do all the days.

Multiple Day Guest Teacher Workshop

This is the same as I just mentioned, but in this scenario you bring in a number of guest teachers to take some classes. This creates a bigger 'wow' factor for your students as the teachers and styles are new and exciting. You're able to charge more for these workshops and again, can include catering in the price.

External Once-Off And Multiple Day Guest Teacher Workshops

We then have external once off and multiple day guest teacher workshops – there's one major word difference in this one, and that word is external. This is a very important difference and I've implemented this strategy with a number of clients who have increased their workshop income and also enrolled new students from running these events. Again, this is a once off workshop for maybe 1.5 hours per age group or level with guest teachers or teacher and is open to the general public. The power is in how you advertise this workshop. Give this workshop a name or if you're using just one high-profile guest teacher, simply use their name. Your studio branding doesn't need to be all over this; instead you create an individual brand for your workshop. You may call it Dynamic Dance Workshop. The venue is your studio, but it's about bringing dancers from all over your area and beyond to this workshop. This is not an exercise in poaching students from other studios – it's a way for you to give back, provide an awesome experience for local dancers and earn additional revenue.

Now, every good studio should have a mixture of all of these. You may run a large external workshop annually so it becomes an important date in everyone's calendar each year, plus a few internal workshops to provide new opportunities to your students while increasing your profit.

We have some great marketing ideas for you to promote your workshops and camps in Chapters 8 and 9, so hold tight!

VIP PROGRAM

This is a new concept in the dance studio world, but one that is really taking off in other industries. Think of Amazon Prime. How could you create additional value for your families through introducing a VIP Program? You could call it Suzie's Dance All Stars, as an example. You would charge an annual fee where your customers (VIP) receive additional benefits for signing up and paying the annual fee. They could receive early bird access to recital/concert tickets, option to have a payment plan for costumes, access to master classes from guest speakers or teachers, discounts on social events, a series of short, must-have warm up stretches for the morning to increase your flexibility, maybe some videos on how to master a triple pirouette. They could go online and look for this, but they want your stuff! They love you and they're your students. Get out a camera and start filming. You could charge anywhere from $50-$200 a year to be part of the annual program.

There you have it. An entire list of additional revenue streams that you could start implementing into your studio today. Sure, it's work up front, but once you create the system and processes, that's it. You create it once and you will see a continual return. Please remember that you don't need to implement all of these into your studio at once, or at all. As I said earlier, it's not about being money hungry or greedy – it's about running a business that makes great profit, while providing an awesome experience for your students and parents.

WHAT'S YOUR NEXT MOVE?

Right now I want you to select two ways you can start either generating new income or further boost your income through one of the strategies you're currently doing, but know you could leverage more if you spend a little more time on it.

Chapter Four

SYSTEMATIZING AND STREAMLINING YOUR ADMINISTRATION PROCESSES

'Systems help us to move forward, to go as far as we possibly can. They enable us to work faster, smarter, and more strategically. A good system eliminates waste, while it also anticipates and removes obstacles. To get the most out of systems, you have to make them a lifestyle, not a one-off deal. They must become ingrained in your routine.' ~ John Maxwell

It was 2am. I had finished teaching at around 9pm, but I was wide awake for hours afterwards as I found myself sending out invoices.

As I sat there, wide awake at 2am, my brain started to churn. One and a half years into owning my dance studio and I thought to myself, 'I'm sitting up at 2am doing billing and invoices. What's happened?'

When I first had the vision to build my dream studio, working at 2am on administrative tasks was not on my vision board. Was it on yours? I doubt it. Then why do so many of us end up being stuck doing things that:

a) Don't grow our businesses
b) Don't fulfil us or bring us joy

The key to unlocking the door and escaping from admin overload, over teaching and being stuck managing loads of staff and teachers is that you need to become an entrepreneur.

After working with hundreds of dance studio owners, I've identified that there are four steps to getting you to entrepreneurial status. Getting to this place is great as you get to do things like:

- Create new income and impact generating projects
- Spend time with your family and friends
- Travel without the studio falling apart
- Work on things that give you energy and make a big difference to your students, parents and teachers

PHASE 1: ADMINISTRATOR

Hands up if you love administration work? (room goes silent, and there's nothing but crickets!) It's a shame that many studio owners can't move through the phase of getting rid of some of the admin tasks in their business, but it happens. All. The. Time. They think, 'I can't afford to give this to someone else,' when the truth is that you can't afford *not* to. You see, admin tasks like invoicing, ordering costumes, responding to basic emails, collating newsletters, liaising with recital/concert venues are low-value tasks. It's not that they're not important, but in terms of money, they are nothing more than $10-$20 per hour tasks. This is not something that the business owner should be doing. Imagine now that you get help for 5-10 hours a week to handle some admin in your business. What high-value tasks could you work on as the business owner in this time? I know – marketing! You then get more hours in the week to work on growing your business and increasing your profits, and that's what will pay for that admin person to help you out.

PHASE 2: TEACHER

In my history of working with studio owners, there's one thing I see all the time – once they start to delegate more of the admin work, they begin to use these 'extra' hours to teach more.

One thing I know without a doubt is that dance studio owners don't need to teach more group classes or private lessons. I've been in your shoes with my own studio. I thought I could save money (expenses) by teaching more classes, which is exactly what I did. I taught about 65% of the classes over about six days a week. The students and parents loved it and so did I. But was this where my limited time was best spent? No. My week was now full to the brim, preparing for classes and teaching dance, all while trying to run my business. There was a staff member in the office now, which was great. I was teaching my little butt off, which also meant that retention was great. But the growth of the studio (new student enrollments) had stunted.

After 12 months of this – making the same money, physically feeling exhausted (damn, I was fit though!), I had to admit to myself, 'Hold up – I'm working my butt off here and the business isn't growing. This doesn't add up!'

As soon as that light bulb started flickering, another epiphany struck. Maybe I should bring in and train some teachers! And in a very short time, that's exactly what I did. Bit by bit, we had new teachers join our faculty. Mind you, I'm not suggesting you employ a whole bunch of teachers and throw them into the classes with no preparation – I've seen many studio owners going from complete control to no control and that's when their business starts to fall apart.

Put a robust teacher recruitment process in place, thoroughly interview potential teachers and put them on a trial where during that time you monitor and mentor them.

PHASE 3: MANAGER

So, your administration is sorted out and you have teachers in place to take much of the load off. So what's next? You become a manager. This phase is one that studio owners find challenging because managing staff is a whole different skill set and you need to learn – quickly – how to effectively:

- Communicate what you want (your vision and values and expectations)
- Communicate what needs improvement (have tough conversations)
- Motivate and inspire to keep staff focused and on track

During this phase there are two things that can happen:

1. You really step into the role of becoming a manager/mentor, which in turn produces teachers that are all about growing their skills to pass onto the students, keeping their passion for always teaching their best class every week and committed to you and your dance families.

2. You let them do whatever they want. They rarely see you or speak with you so there's no connection to the studio, and they turn into that person who's just showing up to get paid. If this happens, you'll know it. You'll start to have a high turnover of staff, and at this point, some teachers may think they can do a better job and start to become your competition, with their own studios. A disconnected studio owner equals a demise in the business.

Hopefully you're the first example and your teachers are going great guns producing awesome results for their students and the studio as a whole. In saying that, you may have a moment, like I did, when you get to the end of the week and see a string of emails and messages from teachers and staff asking loads of questions, changing shifts, and you say, 'I think I need a life outside of the studio.'

So, you start the journey of finding one or two people who can manage your studio on a day-to-day level. A studio manager (operations and business/marketing) and an artistic director (classes and creative ideas) are ideal.

Tip: During the manager stage, you may also have a part time marketing/sales coordinator working for you too. I highly suggest this.

PHASE 4: ENTREPRENEUR

This is where the magic happens. I get goosebumps while I write this as the fourth stage is when you finally get to experience what was on your vision board when you first planned to have your own dance studio.

I've been lucky enough to witness my clients and program members transition through these phases, and I can tell you now that when you step into the role of the entrepreneur, your life and business will shift.

Being a true entrepreneur in your studio means that you get to work on things that really light you up. You'll spend your days working on 'big' ideas to grow your profit and impact in your business. Financial freedom is another positive outcome of reaching this stage, but for me, it's about spending more time with loved ones, travelling and realizing just how much more of an impact you can make on your dance families when everything else is taken care of.

Alert: I should mention here that, as an entrepreneur, you'll still work bloody hard, but as you'll be working on the awesome stuff, it won't feel like work. And yes, you will need to put out some fires along the way. This is all part of the journey and you'll never stop learning!

WHERE ARE YOU?

Where are you currently in your journey to becoming an entrepreneur in your studio? What's next? Once you work out where you are, you'll need to create an action plan full of all the little steps that will get you to that next stage!

Okay, so now you can see the roadmap and the journey to becoming an entrepreneur, let's get you making progress to that place where you and your business are thriving.

When it comes to running a successful studio, there is one thing you need to know: you can't do it alone, which you know now from reading the above. Every day, studio owners tell me that they are working 70 hour weeks and can't afford to employ anyone. My response is always, 'You can't afford not to.'

It doesn't matter whether you're just starting out on your studio owner journey or you're well into the business, you can never stop learning about hiring, training and retaining the right people to help steer your dream and get you hitting those big goals!

The thing is, you're not doing anyone – yourself, the business – any favors by wearing every single hat in your studio. Go down the list and tick the box if you're the one currently doing that role in your studio:

- Dance Teacher
- Receptionist
- Office Manager

- Cleaner
- Bookkeeper
- Marketing Manager
- Costume Coordinator
- Project Manager
- Programs Manager
- Graphic Designer
- Website Designer & Developer
- Copywriter
- Social Media Manager
- Newsletter & Communication Writer
- Clint, I'm Everything!

I get it – that's how most of us start out. And while it's okay to be operating like this for the first year (you need to hustle to bring in those students!) after that point, this shouldn't be the case. You see, as the studio owner you should only be working in your zone of genius, doing only what you do best. Ideally, these are tasks that grow your business – whether it's creating programs, retention strategies or student attraction promotions. These are the tasks that take your business to the next level.

In Chapter 1, you wrote down what your dream day looks like. It's important we now see how far off you are from living that day, as well as pinpoint what you're actually filling your time with each week. I know you're busy, but are you busy doing income generating business growth activities – or are you doing low-value tasks that are just getting your business through day-by-day?

SEVEN-DAY AUDIT

Before we talk about your other support staff and what they need to be doing, you must have absolute clarity on the tasks you're doing, hence why you need to complete a seven-day audit. There's no reason to be afraid – I promise you that once you complete the audit over the next week, you will become a better version of yourself as a leader in your studio.

You can start with a notebook, Excel or Google sheet and map out the next seven days in 30-minute blocks, starting at 6am and ending at

10am. Then I want you to fill in the spaces with what you're working on every half an hour. And that means everything! Think of this as a food diary, only instead of what you eat, you fill in what you do each day.

Once you have completed the audit, after the seven days it's time to go through, review and analyze it. During this time you'll gain clarity on what you've been working on, and if 90% of those tasks are contributing to your 90-day, 6-month and 12-month goals. It's a real eye opener.

Grab a highlighter and go through each task, grouping them into sections. Below is an example:

Yellow – Teaching
Green – Admin Work
Blue – Business Development (marketing and retention)
Red – Management (staff meetings, hiring, training)
Orange – Wasted Time (on social media sites, watching TV)
Purple – Me Time (exercise, meditation, fun things for you)
Pink – Family & Friends Time

You can create categories that work for you, then add up all the hours each week that you spend in each area. This is also similar to a bit of a life audit, so you'll not only get insight into your studio, but insight into you as a human outside of the studio (yes, there is such a thing!).

Once you've done that, it's time to review your goals and start making a plan of how you're going to get to where you want to be, faster. This is generally through hiring staff, to take over admin work or marketing, and creating stricter boundaries around your working or teaching hours so that you can spend more time with loved ones or on your hobbies. Only you will know what is right for you, but this is a great power exercise to highlight what's really going on and to show you where you can make improvements.

As this chapter is all about your office staff and systemizing your administration process, let's jump in.

YOUR ADMINISTRATION STAFF

Whether you have one staff member running your office, a few or maybe it's you, your husband or wife or a family member, there are certain qualities these people need.

I've spoken with thousands of studio owners over the years and sometimes they tell me, 'Clint, it feels like my office staff run my business.' No matter who you have working in the office, they are working for you – you run the show. Please never forget this, for if you want to take your studio to the next level, it's crucial that you have a team who have an all hands on deck mentality.

When I talk about your office staff I'm talking about your office manager, receptionist/s and virtual assistants.

YOUR DREAM LIST

In an ideal world, what would you like your office staff to do? Now I don't want you to think about the person you have currently working for you or how much money they are going to cost, I want you to think about your dream task list for this person. Think about your seven-day audit and all those things you listed that you get caught up with on the admin side of things.

It's important we look at this first as based on the tasks you want the person in the role to do, it will determine the qualities they need to have to be a great fit for your studio! I've created a list of tasks for you below for inspiration that you can tailor to your needs.

Email Management

- Management of studio email address. Being able to respond to enquiries directly
- Deleting SPAM
- Adding all contacts to your chosen software system
- Managing the studio master diary. I suggest you set up Google Calendar for this
- Travel arrangements (business and personal)

Organisation & Administration

- Answering and looking after the studio phone
- Organisation of Dropbox folders and files
- Creating databases through research
- Creating and managing documents in word and excel
- Creating PDF documents

- Transcription of audio and video files
- Creating reports, forms, templates etc
- Online research
- Publishing blog posts (latest news) including adding images, tags and keywords to the website
- Publishing newsletters via Mailchimp and/or Send Pepper
- Moderating blog comments
- Creating and sending invoices through system (Basic book keeping)
- Following up unpaid invoices with clients (Follow process)
- Personal errands for studio owners
- Managing contacts in software program
- Creating new lists in software system and tagging appropriately, as well as adding to correct sequence
- Create new messages and sequences in software system
- Create and schedule emails to go out to specific lists and contacts
- Sending out emails for student birthdays and keeping student birthday documents up to date
- Keep 10 influencers' contacts and latest content up to date
- Managing and tracking monthly financial results through spreadsheets and software system
- Call students (retention calls)
- Order stationary and studio equipment
- Track class attendance
- Compile the weekly report
- Send out exit surveys
- Register for competitions
- Order uniforms and merchandise
- Order items for the shop (food and drinks)

Project & Events Management

- Monitoring potential students moving through the online sales funnel and following up with these people to schedule complimentary lesson
- Researching and booking venues for events (concert, studio days) and organising logistics

- Creating event materials (basic graphic design)
- Monitoring event attendee numbers and scheduling emails
- Set reminder for large projects including promotion dates, going live dates etc
- Costume management for performances and during the concert season

Social Media

- Posting and scheduling Facebook page status updates weekly. Finding content which studio owner then approves
- Creating promotions and offers on Facebook
- Collating Facebook insights monthly and providing a report
- Create and manage LinkedIn Account
- Creating images (branded quotes) and posting to Instagram
- Manage Instagram account
- Manage YouTube Account by uploading videos weekly
- Moderate YouTube comments
- Answer questions and inquiries from users across all social media accounts. Ask Studio Owner if you need assistance.
- Identify online groups to share content (across social media, blogs, online communities)

Website

- Keyword research
- Designing landing pages through lead pages
- Support and develop wordpress website pages
- Website maintenance
- Creating backlinks
- Basic SEO work

Other

- Basic photoshop editing skills (resizing, change file format etc)
- Removing background noise from audio and video
- Create and monitor Facebook Adverts
- Create and monitor Google Adwords accounts

- Finding other online platforms or websites to host content (newsletters, videos, blogs, be a guest blogger podcasts etc)
- Managing partner relationships
- Looking for new partner relationships
- Google Analytics monthly report

Important Qualities To Flourish

So now you have seen just some of what your office staff members can do for you, let's look at the qualities this person needs to really thrive in your studio. Your office staff are the action takers in your studio so it's important you support, train them efficiently and let them know that you're always there if they need you. Ongoing training is also crucial for them to be a superstar in their role.

Qualities to look for when it comes to hiring office staff:

- High attention to detail
- Resilient
- Persistent
- Good organizer
- Highly organized
- Loves people
- Ability to teach others
- Excellent communication skills
- Passion for a high level of service
- Patience
- Honesty
- Excellent listener
- Eagerness to learn new things and to be challenged
- Able to create team spirit
- Calm and confident in all situations
- Constantly in touch with the new facts and methods to increase their efficiency

I believe these are the core qualities that make for a successful office staff member. You may have a few more you'd like to include when hiring or revisiting the tasks for your current office staff.

Who Should You Hire?

When it comes to hiring an office staff member, I often get asked whether it's better to find someone who is already part of the family (like a mother, student or a family member) or hire someone completely independent. In an ideal world you want to engage someone who has no previous connection with the studio, yet has an interest and/or knowledge of dance and a dance studio. This can be hard to find sometimes, but on most occasions my clients have recruited someone who fits this profile.

There are many reasons why hiring from within isn't ideal and for me, the person who is in the office should be as neutral as possible – at the end of the day, they are there to do an amazing job while also having a good time.

If you're just starting out, you may want to start with someone just 5-10 hours a week to help you get through admin tasks, which will allow you time to work on the business instead of in it. If you already have a few staff working for you in the business on the office side then assess their roles and take it from there.

The most important thing I can say about office staff is that, just like your teachers, you need to invest time into them. Block out times during the week to train them, answer their questions and build a solid relationship. They are the heartbeat of your studio and keep your business operating on the day-to-day level.

MY FAVORITE ONLINE TOOLS TO HAVE YOUR OFFICE OPERATING AT ITS BEST

The world has gone digital. There are literally millions of business tools that you can use to operate and grow your dance studio. After years of research and testing, here is my list of the five essential online business tools that I have found vital to running your studio well and with ease.

Google Drive

Google Drive is a 'cloud' storage location that is free for up to 15 GB. Cloud storage is where you store information off site and off of your computer.

For studio owners, this has several advantages over storing data and files on your computers hard drive:

Sharing documents – You can share documents with your teachers, students, and parents easily. It is as simple as entering an email or sending everyone a link to the item. Documents like studio newsletters, flyers, and more can all be shared very easily.

Safe storage – Because your data is in the cloud, you don't need to worry if your computer crashes. All of your information is kept safely in a place where a faulty computer can't hurt it. This makes it easier to ensure the continuity of your business, even if your primary computer dies.

Easy access – With Google Drive you can access your files from anywhere in the world. As long as you have internet access, you can get to your files on almost any device. This means that you can work from anywhere that has Wi-Fi access. Being a studio owner is a full-time job and Google Drive can make it easy to work from anywhere you are.

Slack

Communicating with your team is very important. Slack makes it easy. Not only can you send messages, you can also upload all kinds of files. You can create channels for separate projects and invite people to those channels. Our members use their channels to organize costumes, recitals, enrollment etc.

As a studio owner, you have lots of information to share from music lists to schedules to new student information. Slack makes it very simple to share and discuss these items and will eliminate all those back and forth emails. Since the teachers at your studio probably work on different schedules, you can even host meetings so that everyone can attend. Keeping your entire team informed is an important key to continuing to employ great teachers.

Asana

Project management is important to guaranteeing that all of your projects are completed well. Asana is an online project management program that lets you work with everyone directly, laying out the stages of a project and making it simple to check off 'to do' lists.

As a studio owner, you probably always have projects coming up. Dance recitals, open houses, and new student drives are just the beginning. Every event has multiple steps. If you have been doing this a while, you are used to doing everything yourself. With Asana, you can plan out the steps and assign them to members of your team, parents, and even students. Everyone will know what they need to do and they can keep you posted on progress.

LeadPages

A landing page is a single page website that usually promotes a single item, event, or offering. LeadPages has hundreds of templates that make it easy to create a new page for almost anything, from an upcoming recital to a new class offering.

I have found that using landing pages is a fast and effective way to market new offerings. New class pages can be set up without any programming experience. The biggest advantage is that you don't need to change your main website every time you want to offer a new product or service. For example, if you are creating a new adult class, you can make a simple landing page and just put a link on your main website. Your marketing materials for the class can just send people directly to the landing page.

GetResponse

Email marketing is an amazing way to keep people informed, make more sales, and maintain relationships with customers.

With GetResponse, you can automate your enrollment process. If someone is interested in learning more, they put in their email address and the system will automatically send out emails for you.

You can use it to answer new student enquiries and for the on-boarding of students. It is also an excellent way to communicate with former students and retain current students by keeping lines of communication open.

For a dance studio, you can use it to answer new student enquiries and for the on boarding of students. It is also an excellent way to communicate with former students and retain current students by keeping lines of communication open.

Filling Your Business Tool Box with the Right tools

These five online tools can make life as a dance studio owner much easier. The fact that you can access them from anywhere means that you are never out of touch with your current students or prospective students. Your staff are able to communicate with you and each other at any time. Saving your data and files is like an insurance policy on your most valuable asset, data.

THE NEW WAY OF RUNNING AN EFFICIENT OFFICE

Now, if you're anything like I was when I started my studio, I wasn't really thinking about implementing a management system into my studio. We had everything on Microsoft Excel and pieces of paper and books! It worked for us... or so I thought. Over the last 10+ years I've certainly found that if you want to spend more time working on than in your business, then implementing a software program to manage the business side of your studio is one of the best things you can do!

Before you say that this looks like a whole bunch of work, know that the programs I want to share with you today have killer customer service! They will spend time with you on the phone and take you through the whole process, step by step.

I know you didn't start your dance studio to be doing administrative work 80% of the time. What a software management program will do, is allow you to have a life and your office staff to work on higher value tasks. When you select the right one for your studio, it will mean that your business will run more efficiently, effectively and productively! Whether you have 30 students or 3,000 students, a management solution is exactly what you need.

Dance Studio Software That Works

At least a few times each week, studio owners ask about what software is best. The thing is, every dance studio is different and every studio has different priorities in terms of what they want their studio software to do. I've put together a list of my five favorite software programs below that you should definitely trial and look into.

- Jack Rabbit
- DanceBiz
- Dance Studio Pro
- Studio Director
- Studio Pulse

Systems Are Really EVERYTHING!

We've spoken a lot about people when it comes to having your office and administration running smoothly in your business, but what it all comes down to is creating systems in your business – creating it once and using it over and over again in your studio.

Every task within your office, in fact, your entire business, can be systemized, and if you're a studio owner who keeps everything in their head then it's time you get it all out of there – and develop systems for your business which will allow you more time off from the studio.

Your studio can be made up of hundreds of systems including:

- How to take a new student enquiry
- How to upload a new blog to the website
- How to post a photo to your Facebook page
- How to take student measurements for costumes
- How to respond to a parent complaint via email

Whether you have office staff or not, I suggest you block out five hours one week to write down all the systems you have in your studio, and another five hours the following week to review those systems. From here, make a plan of when you or your staff will create each system. It's a slow and steady process, but one that not many studio owners do because it takes time. It sure does, but if you want to grow and eventually sell your studio, your systems are a big asset to your business – without them, you won't see sustainable growth nor will you be able to spend time away from the studio without problems arising. One of my favorite books on building a successful business through systems is *The E-Myth* by Michael Gerber. My favorite quote from this author? 'Build systems within each business function. Let systems run the business and people run the systems. People come and go but the systems remain constant.'

Chapter Five

RECRUITING & TRAINING YOUR ALL STAR FACULTY

'When people are financially invested, they want a return.
When people are emotionally invested, they want to contribute.'
~ Simon Sinek

Your teachers are the backbone of your business. Without the right teachers teaching the right classes in the right styles, your studio won't be operating at its full potential. It took me a few years to realize that I didn't need to teach every class in my studio for it to thrive – quite the opposite, in fact. It was only when I brought in strong and passionate teachers that the studio really started to flourish!

What are the key qualities you're looking for when hiring a new teacher? I'm sure you're looking for a bunch of things: past experience, age, location, whether they are reliable, will they stay long term, are they going to be committed to the growth of the students, have they got any formal qualifications, can they entertain and inspire my students, what do they post on social media, can they handle feedback, are they open to further training, will they want to become part of your dance family. The list goes on!

You see, every dance studio has their own list of values and as a studio owner, you have your own expectations of what you want from a teacher.

3 CORE CATEGORIES

I've made this process as simple and effective as possible, having fine-tuned it over the years. There are three core categories you want to explore when identifying what it is you really need and want in a teacher, including:

1. ATTRIBUTES

Over the years the five top teacher attributes I've found from working in my own studio and with other studios across the globe are:

Energy – Your teachers need to be energetic from the moment they walk into the studio to the moment they walk out the door. While I'm not a fan of saying, 'leave your problems at the door,' as a dance teacher, you have to. You need to walk into that class each and every time and deliver the most energetic and content-rich class of your life. When your students are having a great time and feeding off your energy, they'll learn faster and their happiness levels will increase. Being energetic is a crucial quality for a teacher to have.

Patience – We've all been a dance student before and remember those teachers who use to fly off the handle if we chatted in class or didn't get the step right after a few attempts. If there are a few students in the room who are struggling, the teacher needs to be able to break things down and quickly adapt their teaching style to suit all skill levels. There's nothing worse than going home as a student and feeling like a failure because the teacher told you off for not getting a step. One of the most helpful things a teacher can do for these students is nurture them, commend them on their efforts, ask them to go home and assure them that getting it right takes time.

Investment – Are your teachers invested in the growth of your students? This is a hard one to identify in an interview or trial class and will take at least a month to really see this first hand. I'm sure you've seen a teacher take a class where it's almost like they're the only one in the room, as they spend the whole time looking at themselves in the mirror admiring how good they are. A teacher should be selfless in the class room; they are there to serve the needs of the students in the class. It's such an awesome feeling as a studio owner to walk into a class where the teacher is 100% present and has completely lost themselves in the students and the class – that's when the magic happens. That's when each student goes home feeling like they were the only ones in the class. That's when you build your tribe.

Consistency – In any business, the ability to be consistent with the delivery of your products and services is important. It's a little trickier when it's a human delivering an experience to another human, such as teaching dance. When I talk about consistency, I'm talking about the teacher turning up for every class the same way. Think about your close group of friends for a moment... Do you have a friend who is one of these people that one day they're your best friend, happy, loving life and texting and calling you, and the next week you don't hear from them, they are down in the dumps and you think you've done something wrong? Most of us have people in our life like this, but this is not what we want in a teacher – and this links back to the energy piece. Students will get the most from their class when there is routine and consistency, especially from the teacher who is taking them.

Role Model – Whether we know it or not, we all have role models, and as children we are always assessing what we want to be when we grow up. I remember being about 13 or 14 and having the most amazing dance teacher who ticked all the boxes when it came to these top five attributes. She was from London and taught our class jazz and tap. Her name was Kelly and she inspired me not only to be an amazing dancer, but to live my life out loud. She had worked with top artists as a dancer in London, and she had this great outlook on life. Every time I walked into class, I was inspired to be a better dancer and a better person. She certainly impacted my life and continues to today. As little people growing up, our teachers can really shape the person we become. Having a bunch of terrific role models in your studio will increase your numbers, increase retention but more importantly, produce outstanding human beings on all levels.

As you can see, within these five main attributes there are many qualities that lie in between including honesty, the ability to communicate effectively, loyalty, support, nurture, inspire, build relationships and many more.

2. EXPERIENCE

My views on a teacher's experience don't sit well with some people, but until I'm proven wrong, I'll keep spreading my message about the experience I believe teachers need, and this is certainly dependent on the ages, styles and levels they are teaching. I don't believe that your teachers need any type of formal qualification like a degree or diploma. I think it's crucial that all of your teachers have a solid technical foundation in the style or styles they're teaching, but all a certificate says is, 'I know some stuff, was dedicated to finish a course and now need some real life experience applying what I learnt into the real world.' It's awesome if they do have a formal qualification as your parents will love this, but they'll love an energetic, patient, invested, consistent teacher their child looks up to as a role model more. In an ideal world, teaching experience is important, but if they haven't had much but they're hungry, show promise and you have time to mentor them and monitor their classes, give them a go. Bring them on as a class cover to start and go from there.

3. ASPIRATIONS

When looking for a new teacher, it's important that you get clarity on their aspirations as a teacher and/or performer. You both need to be on the same page in terms of their career and your expectations. Do they want to go overseas and dance on a cruise ship in three months' time? Do they want to be a dance teacher full-time and want to make a real difference to a studio? Do they want to have a baby in a year's time? Find out what their aspirations are at that moment. I acknowledge that the difficult thing about aspirations is that they're ever-changing, but my biggest tip here is to ensure you have a very open door policy with your teachers so that when they do change, you're the first to know – not the last.

There you have it: the three core categories to explore when looking for teachers to build your amazing faculty.

You will see here that I don't mention age. Over my years working with studios I have found that there are certain qualities you find in older teachers that could be missing or not as present as in younger teachers, but this also goes both ways. I strongly believe that if you identify what you want and need from the three main categories, experience, attributes and aspirations, age is irrelevant. I've seen this theory proven over and over again with my private mentoring clients.

I'm passionate about people and I hope this lesson has inspired you to be clear on what it is you actually want in a teacher. Once you go through and identify what this looks like for you and your studio, take some time to go through your current teaching faculty to see if there are teachers you might need to sit down with and have a proper one-on-one conversation with to address some of your concerns. It's certainly not about telling them that they now need to be more energetic or whatnot – it's about listening and sharing your current observations and working out some new ways of doing this. More on this coming up!

WHERE TO FIND THE BEST TEACHERS FOR YOUR STUDIO

So where do you currently advertise for teachers? Most of the studios I've worked with over the years always answer this question with word of mouth. Let's jump straight into all the places you can uncover new teachers.

1. Directly from resumés emailed to you – Have you ever had a resumé sent to you via email or post from a teacher interested in working for you? This is awesome as it has come directly to you and the person has taken the effort to reach out. I encourage all of my clients to have a short paragraph on their contact page on their website that says:

Interested in teaching for us? We're always on the lookout for passionate, energetic and experienced teachers to join our rock star faculty. If you're interested in teaching please email us your resumé detailing your experience. We'd also love to hear from you in at least 250 words why you'd like to join our inspiring team of teachers. We look forward to hearing from you!

By giving them that little writing task you won't hear from the teachers who are looking to make a quick buck – you'll only receive applications from people who are serious about the role. You can also hear that this short paragraph sounds quite exciting and really makes applicants want to be part of the team. It sounds like somewhere they want to be. When you receive any resumés, always reply promptly with an email thanking them for their application and letting them know you'll be in touch regarding the next steps. Have a look at the application and see if you think they could be a good fit. I always encourage my clients to have a 15-minute initial telephone interview before a face-to-face interview and trial class – or putting the resumé in the bin.

2. Recommendations – Make people in your community aware that you're always on the lookout for great new teaching talent – your parents, students, strategic partners, family... basically everyone you know. Although you won't be needing new teachers every day, why limit your opportunity to hear from awesome teachers just when you're looking – this means you cast the net very shallow. You can always have them as a teacher to cover classes and then, if they're great, wait for a more permanent opportunity to arise. A few of my students have really risen the bar when it comes to teacher recommendations and we have introduced a very simple teacher referral program, where if someone refers a teacher to the studio and that teacher is brought on board, the referring family receives a gift voucher for $100. Depending on where you are in the world, this needs to be relevant, but I think $100 for finding an awesome teacher that could make you thousands of dollars is a prime investment! This is a killer strategy and also increases your brand awareness as people will be talking about how your studio is always looking for the best teachers! Awesome!

3. Talk to your dance studio owner friends – As a dance studio owner it's important to build a network of other like-minded people, which includes other studio owners. I'm not saying you need to be friends with the studio owner up the road – they might be in another city or a few miles or kilometres away. Ask them if they have come across any awesome teachers who they would recommend. Sure, some won't give away their secrets, but you'd be surprised how many will open up to you if you've already built the relationship.

4. Contact companies – Reach out to dance companies in your city who are working with amazing dancers and see if they have any teachers who are keen and available. You would be surprised how many beautiful dance teachers come from ballet and contemporary companies – not to mention all the knowledge and technique they can pass on to your students!

5. Social media – Do you have a Facebook page, personal profile, Instagram account or similar? Simply put the word out there that you're looking for teachers (use the paragraph from the contact page on your website) and encourage your communities to share and let their circle of contacts know. Direct them to the contact page so they can follow the same process to apply. Now, if you want to be really clever and have a small amount of money to invest, why not run an advertisement on Facebook? This is another great way to generate more new teacher leads.

6. Online resources – Thanks to the world of online there are many directories, forums, magazines, job boards, job websites that you can post on and most of them are for free. Many of the online dance resources have job boards or will include your paragraph about seeking teachers in their EDM (electronic direct mail) or newsletter. Create a list of the online platforms in your city that you could approach to work with on having a continual presence. The other idea that I suggest to my private clients is to write a few articles for these online dance publications around teaching and at the end add your bio line and some copy about you always looking for dedicated, energetic and passionate teachers and put your contact link there. The great thing about articles is that they are online forever, positions you as an authority plus all it costs you is the time to write the article and a small fee for a copywriter to edit it.

7. Colleges and full-time schools – Colleges and full-time performing arts or dance schools are popping out graduates all the time so it makes perfect sense for you to form relationships with these education institutes so that you're their first point of call. I even have some of my private clients come in to these studios and talk about how to become a dance teacher and the life of a dance studio owner. It's special to be able

to mentor and educate our upcoming talent on the opportunities that are out there besides being a back-up dancer for artists. Definitely make a list of your local colleges and start building a relationship.

There are teachers out there, you just need to look for them and focus on exactly who you are after! You'll be surprised when you put this recruitment process in place how many amazing teachers will be knocking down your door!

THE 3 STEP TEACHER INTERVIEW PROCESS

It's one thing to have an awesome resumé and be a great dancer, but being an amazing and engaging teacher who is right for your studio is another thing. Hence why you need to go through a thorough 3 step interview process.

1. Telephone Interview
2. Face-to-Face Interview
3. Have them conduct a minimum of two trial classes

Telephone Interview

Let's talk about the telephone interview. Once you receive their resumé and have decided that you'd like to learn more, send them an email giving them three dates and times you're available for a telephone interview. You may even want to use Timetrade to schedule these appointments. This awesome online tool allows people to book meetings with you in your diary. In this email ask for the best number for you to call them on and say it will only take about 15 minutes. You also want to ask them to confirm the best date and time within 24 hours. This should always be done via email as it's the first part of the process. Just from this email, you will start to get a sense of what this person is like. You will see how quickly they come back to you, the tone and excitement in the email, whether they provide you all the details you needed including confirmation of the date and time as well as their number. Once they confirm, make sure you place their details in your diary and call them right on time.

In the telephone interview, your only objective is simple. Do you like them? Some people will say that this approach is harsh and that you need to give people a go... Unfortunately, first impressions last when it comes to new teachers, parents and students. Here are the three things you want to cover in the phone interview:

Why you? – They may be nervous, so make sure you ease them into the conversation and set the scene. You just wanted to have a casual chat and get to know them more as a person. Ask how their day or week was. This is only 15 minutes, so don't get too bogged down in the detail. The first question you want to ask them is, 'Sally, I really appreciated you contacting us about joining our teaching family. I'd love to hear a little more from you on why you'd make a great addition to our teaching team here at Explosion Dance Academy.' In their answer, you'll be listening for information on the three core categories of what you want in a teacher… attributes, experience and ambition. If you don't receive information on all three, dig a bit deeper. End that part with something along the lines of, 'Awesome Sally, thank you for sharing that with me, sounds great.' Keep it light and positive so it doesn't impact the rest of the interview.

Why us? – Next you want to find out why are they applying to your studio. You ask this for two reasons, the main reason being to truly understand why they want to work for you. The second is to gauge how you're perceived in the market – which doubles as a little feedback for you, which I love. You might ask, 'So Sally, there are quite a few dance studios around the area – why us? Why would you like to come and work with our dynamite teaching team?' Listen closely to see if the picture she paints of your studio is actually how it operates. You'll be getting a great sense for who Sally is now.

What next? – There are two things that can happen next. If you're not interested in going any further with the candidate, you can either:

a) thank them for their time and say that you'll be leaving their resumé on file for when a suitable teaching position becomes available, or
b) be honest with them and let them know why you're not moving forward with the process. Give them feedback but also some tips on how they could improve for next time. There are a gazillion reasons why you may not want to move forward so make it relevant, helpful and inspiring feedback.

If you want to move forward to a face-to-face interview and trial classes, the last question you want to ask is, 'Sally, what do you think should be our next steps together?' This question throws most people and I don't ask this to intentionally throw them off course. I ask this question to see how they answer it. You see, as a teacher they will be asked all types of unexpected questions and need to think quickly and come up with an answer. Of course their answer generally won't determine if you'll move them to the next stage or not, as you've decided you will. Ideally you want them to say, 'Well Clint, I've really enjoyed our short chat today and I'd love to continue speaking with you about how I could be a great asset to your studio. For me, it would be great for us to meet face-to-face plus I'd like to show you my teaching style by taking a trial class or two.' If that was their answer, I'd hire them on the spot! No, in all seriousness, listen to what they are after and then suggest that you do have a face-to-face 45-minute interview followed by, ideally, two trial classes. Lock in the date and time with them right there on the phone and send a follow-up email confirming the details, including the structure of the trial class.

Face-to-Face Interview

Okay, before we jump into how to run an effective trial with a potential teacher, let's get into the nuts and bolts of running the face-to-face interview. This is really just an extension of the phone interview but here is where you can get down to the facts. You don't need to go over what they explained to you in the telephone interview. Here's your face-to-face interview questions:

The Questions:

- What gets you out of bed each morning?
  This may seem like a random question, but this question is going to allow them to relax and tap straight into the reason they love their life, giving them the opportunity to drop the nerves and answer your questions the best way possible.
- Tell me about your training and teaching experience to date? What styles are your favorite to teach? Have you completed your exams in any particular syllabus?
- What do you love most about teaching?
- What challenges do you think come with being a dance teacher?

- What age group do you find you connect with most on a teaching level?
- Are you currently working and/or studying? Please tell me more about your other time commitments? This would include teaching at any other studios.
- If we were to move forward together and have you as a teacher at our studio, what commitment could you provide us with in terms of availability? Days and times?
- Tell me about why you left your last two teaching positions? This is only relevant if they have taught before.
- Depending on the classes you would take, there is occasionally other times you'd be required to be at the studio including additional rehearsals, concerts, recitals, performances, faculty meetings, teacher training etc. We will always give you as much notice as possible when these things come up. How do you feel about these additional commitments? This is quite an open question so you can get honest feedback.
- How would the students you've previously taught describe your classes?
- How would the past studio owners you've worked for describe your teaching style?
- When teaching a dance class what are your top three objectives for the students in that class?
- What or who inspired you on a personal and professional level?
- How do you think you transfer that inspiration through to your students?
- Students can sometimes be challenging. Tell me about two examples of where you've handled a difficult child in class?
- Why do you love teaching?
- What aspect of teaching do you least enjoy?
- Social media plays a bit part of our lives in terms of connecting with others. How do you manage the student/teacher relationship online?
- What are your professional goals over the next three months, six months, 12 months, three years?
- Have you completed a working with children check before, ever been committed of a crime or hold a visa that doesn't allow you to work in (country name).

Once you have finished the interview ensure you ask them if they have any questions. Next step? The trial classes.

The Trial Classes

The trial process will alter slightly depending on if you're looking for a permanent teacher now or a cover teacher, or if you'll have them teach one particular style or a few. I always encourage my clients to pay the teacher for their trial classes. The amount is up to you and should be in line with your current teachers' hourly wage.

In regards to the trial class, I suggest you have them take two age groups in one style or two depending on what you want them to teach. The most effective structure of a one-hour trial class I've found works with my clients follows this process.

5 minutes – Introduce teacher and have them tell a bit of their dance story to date. It's important that the students can connect with the teacher and find them relevant. This creates buy-in from the students and gives the teacher the best chance to give a brilliant class.

10 minutes – Warm up. Here you want to be watching their energy levels, knowledge of the human body and how they are explaining and teaching the students about the movement they are doing. A fantastic dance teacher will not only demonstrate the movement, but explain why you're doing the movement and how it should feel.

15 minutes – 1 x technical combination (depending on the style this can be from anywhere in the room – have them mix it up: corner work, floor work). Give them flexibility here but you want them to demonstrate their knowledge of technique.

25 minutes – Main Combination – Here you want them to deliver a piece of choreography of about 30 seconds (depending on the style and intricacies of the choreography). Again, here observe their teaching style, but more importantly how the students are reacting.

5 minutes – tell the teacher to take a 5-minute break outside and sit with the students to get their feedback. This is important for two reasons – you get the thoughts of your students straight away, plus the students feel even more a part of the studio. They feel like they have a say, which is important. You would then have the teacher come back and take the second trial class if that's what you've arranged.

Feedback Time

At the end of the trials sit down with the teacher for five minutes and give them feedback on their class. Firstly, ask them how they felt, what they really enjoyed and if there is anything they could have improved. Then give them feedback. The process for this is to tell them:

a) what you really loved in their teaching
b) what they could think about for next time
c) what you loved about them as a person. This is an excellent way to wrap it up and you'll be able to see how well they take feedback and if they have experience in reflecting on the learnings and applying them to their next class.

Be Thankful

From here, let them know that you'll be in touch within a certain time period and thank them again for coming in. No matter what the outcome is, I would encourage you to send them a handwritten card in the mail to say thank you. This will come from a place of being grateful and also gives them a sense of how you treat your teachers, plus they won't feel negative towards you and the studio if you don't take them on board.

Follow Up

Follow up with the teacher within seven days to let them know how you want to move forward or not. This should always be done via phone and followed up with an email.

As I mentioned earlier, your teachers are your backbone to the business. Yes, you are paying them to do a job, you have a business because of them – so be thankful and show the love... even at times when you want to rip out your hair!

WHAT TO PAY YOUR TEACHERS

The fees that you pay your teachers always comes up with studio owners I speak with and, to be honest, there is no right or wrong financial model. It's really about what works for both parties. You want a very fair fee structure for your teachers, that's consistent and rewards them where appropriate, yet doesn't leave your bank account empty!

As a business owner you want to ensure you're running a lean expenses machine, but you don't want to skimp on your teacher's fees, or get low-quality teachers and have students leave. It's making sure that the teachers you're employing aren't just doing it for the money (the three-step interview process will widdle these people out) and that they have a fire inside of them bigger than just wanting their money at the end of the week. Although we all need money to survive, right?

So what financial models are out there for paying your regular teachers that keeps your teaching faculty feeling appreciated without sending you broke? That's exactly what I'm going to be discussing with you in this chapter, but first there is one important – actually, I say mandatory – thing with my private mentoring clients, and that's the fact that most problems with teachers occur because you assume one thing and they assume another. Basically, you're not on the same page and never have been as you don't have a teacher contract. Teacher contracts are an important piece of giving the studio owner and teacher relationship the best possible chance at thriving. So once you decide to hire a teacher the next thing you want to do is send them a contract outlining how the relationship will work along with clearly outlining expectations. This way everyone is on the same page the majority of the time.

Every country has different laws when it comes to how you contract staff and what can be included and not included. Also, your teachers may be a contractor or employee hence these people would be treated differently. Any contract should be looked over by a lawyer, but for now, let's go through the key points you may like to include in your teachers contract:

Their Position

It's clear to outline exactly what they'll be engaged to do as a teacher at your studio along with any benefits they'll receive, insurances they must hold and who owns the copyright to the work they produce for you. Copyright is a big one as I have seen teachers move from studio to studio teaching the same routines and this can become a challenge.

Schedule

Outline their teaching schedule and mention the fact that it will change depending on enrolled numbers. Also outline the holiday periods and any other times when they won't be needed or needed in addition to their regular classes. This could be for performance rehearsals, concerts or recitals etc. Spell this out very clearly.

Ethics and Values

You can list the ethics and values of the studio here and also what you expect from a teacher in this area. If you've gone through the entire teacher recruitment process then these should match up nicely.

Non Compete

This section is really about what you feel comfortable with. You may put restrictions on where else they can work and that they can teach at another studio but it has to be outside of a certain mile or kilometre radius.

Payment Terms

Here is where you would outline their pay rate as well as when they will be paid.

Now then, let's talk about how you are paying your staff.

When it comes to paying your teachers you need to ask yourself a few questions first:

- How much experience does the teacher have?
- How much of an impact will this teacher have on my bottom line?
- What profit are these classes currently making for the business and what's the opportunity to increase the profit per class?

There are three main models for paying your teachers:

1. Graded Hourly Rate
2. Graded Hourly Rate + Per Student Commission
3. Per Student Commission Only

As I mentioned there is no right or wrong answer here and not all models will work for your studio.

Graded Hourly Rate

The graded hourly rate model gives teachers a flat hourly rate depending on their experience. Please don't pay too much attention to the prices here. The price will be dependent on where your studio is located, the size of your studio and your offering.

Grade 1: Student Teacher: $20 per hour
Grade 2: Assistant Teacher (2 or 3 years as a student teacher): $25 per hour
Grade 3: Graduate Teacher (16+): $35 per hour
Grade 4: Associate Teacher (18+ and 2 years + experience): $45 per hour
Grade 5: Advanced Teacher (18+ and 3 year + experience): $55 per hour
Grade 6: Professional Teachers (4 years + experience): $65 per hour

This is a very simple model that certainly has its pros and cons. Pros are that it's very easy to process from an administration side of things and the biggest downside to this model is that a teacher may see all the students turning up for their class and they are only getting X amount and you're making X amount. As an example, say you have 25 students in one class, who are each paying $15. They calculate that you're making $375 from that class and you're paying them $45 per hour. This may not seem fair to them and feel like you're taking advantage of them, which is why the per student commission model may assist in retention as well as boosting new student numbers as the teachers are incentivized to building their class numbers.

Graded Hourly Rate + Per Student Commission

Basically you're saying to the teacher, run your classes like it's your own studio without the headache of administration and parents.

In this example below, you will see that I have dropped the hourly rate by $5 and there is no commission for student or assistant teachers.

Grade 1: Student Teacher: $20 per hour
Grade 2: Assistant Teacher (2 or 3 years as a student teacher): $25 per hour
Grade 3: Graduate Teacher (16+): $30 per hour + $1.00 per student per

hour from 5 students
Grade 4: Associate Teacher (18+ and 2 years + experience): $40 per hour + $1.00 per student per hour from 5 students
Grade 5: Advanced Teacher (18+ and 3 year + experience): $50 per hour + $1.50 per student per hour from 5 students
Grade 6: Professional Teachers (4 years + experience): $60 per hour + $1.50 per student per hour from 5 students

This is a great model for incentivizing your teachers while they still feel secure by getting a base hourly wage. Again, the figures will depend on your location as well as what you can afford. Remember this doesn't have to be set in concrete – you can trial it for six months to see how it works for you and the teachers. The downside to this model is it requires a little more administration and accounting work as class numbers can fluctuate regularly.

Per Student Commission Only

The last model is the per student commission fee only. This means that there is no base hourly rate and your teachers are paid from the first student. I don't like to introduce this model until you get to the graduate teacher level. Remember, these prices are only an example as it's dependent on your location and the amount of children you can take in a class.

Grade 1: Student Teacher: $20 per hour
Grade 2: Assistant Teacher (2 or 3 years as a student teacher): $25 per hour
Grade 3: Graduate Teacher (16+): $6.00 per student per hour for the first student and $2.00 per hour per student after that
Grade 4: Associate Teacher (18+ and 2 years + experience): $7.00 per student per hour for the first student and $2.50 per hour per student after that
Grade 5: Advanced Teacher (18+ and 3 year + experience): $8.00 per student per hour for the first student and $3.00 per hour per student after that
Grade 6: Professional Teachers: $9.00 per student per hour for the first student and $3.50 per hour per student after that

So there are the rates you'll pay your teachers for lessons, but what about other things including recital and concert rehearsals, performances, performance rehearsals, open days and open houses, staff meetings and training days? There are no set rates for these. I have worked with studio owners who have paid a higher rate to their teachers that takes into account these additional commitments and others who pay per hour or per day for these additional commitments. Again, there is no right or wrong answer here. As long as it's all set out in your teacher's contract, then you'll each be on the same page.

GUEST TEACHERS

The only other thing that may come up is how much you pay for a guest teacher to come and teach a group or solo routine for your students. The amounts you will pay will depend on the person but as an example you may pay a guest teacher $700 for a group routine (7 hours) and $350 for a solo number (3 hours). If they are out of town you will need to cover their travel expenses including transportation, transfers and accommodation as well as a daily per diem for food and drink. My clients have been caught in the past as they have booked all the logistics, then the teacher pulls out last minute and the studio loses the money. The best idea here is to give the teacher a travel budget for all the logistics on top of their fee and have them book it. This way you're not going to lose any money if they pull out.

At the end of the day the important key takeaways here are that your teachers are being paid fairly for the work they are doing and you're running a profitable business.

RECRUITING ROCKSTAR TEACHERS THAT STAY

Having clear expectations and KPIs (key performance indicators) for your teachers is crucial if you want to continue increasing the quality of training and experience in class for your students. In this chapter I'll share with you how to have your teachers taking responsibility and being accountable so that they turn up to each lesson running their class as if it was their own business. Plus, we'll discuss how to keep your top teachers around without opening up their own studio around the corner.

Do you have any KPIs for your teachers? Do you make them accountable for retaining numbers? How about giving them due dates for when routines need to be finished? Do you meet with your teachers regularly on a semi-formal basis to discuss their performance and address any concerns or challenges they have? Having an open door policy for your teachers where you're available to speak with them and mentor them will certainly assist in creating teachers that go above and beyond, increase student numbers and keep your current students loving your studio.

Step #1 – Layout Your KPIs

So the first thing you need to do is layout a list of Key Performance Indicators (KPIs) for your teachers. These will come from the list of expectations that you've set in your teacher contract and will also form the basis for regular reviews you do with your teachers.

In terms of teacher reviews, you should do this at least twice a year. I prefer it is done on a once a quarter basis, as six months is a long time to go without a formal meeting. I'm sure you catch up with your teachers regularly, but most of the time other people are around so it's difficult for them and you to discuss things that could be sensitive. Schedule these dates in the calendar at the beginning of the new year so they are locked in the diary.

KEEPING YOUR AWESOME TEACHING FACULTY

Many studio owners I work with privately are always worried about retaining their top teachers. This is a concern for business owners across all industries. The solution is simple… if you want to keep your top teachers you need to keep two things top of mind.

Be Their Mentor

You need to be their mentor – It's in your best interests that your teachers are continually growing both personally and professionally so they can pass all their knowledge and experience on to your students. You should look at yourself as a mentor for your teachers. Your door should always be open to support them and assist them in their growth as a person and as a dance teacher. By having this front of mind and acting on it, you'll certainly be a studio that teachers will be lining up to work for. As a mentor it's not about always giving them the answers, and I'm not saying that they should come running to you every time there is a problem. Train your teachers to deal with small challenges that come up in class, in class, but if there's a larger or recurring issue, let them know that your door is always open. You want them to present you with at least one solution when they come to you with the problem. You then act like a sounding board and assist them with coming up with the best solution possible.

Manage Your Teachers

The next thing you need to do is manage your teachers. I can tell you now that if you have a teacher contract in place with both of your expectations explained clearly, you shouldn't have to spend much time managing your teachers. In saying this, they do need the regular check points throughout the term or month to speak with you and for you both to catch up. Again, this is not the wave hello through the window before they start class and the same when they leave. You should be catching up formally at least every six weeks. This ideally should be in person, or if not via phone or Skype. This provides you and them the opportunity to go through the great things and possibly the not so great things. You need to address the good and the bad in these catch ups. Over the years I've worked with a number of studio owners who avoid confrontation at all costs. Unfortunately, by doing this your business could be falling away. I really don't know any human who enjoys confrontation, but as a business owner the hard conversations have to be had to ensure your business is still here tomorrow.

Some studio owners are at the studio every day and night while some aren't. If you have less contact with your teachers it's time to step it up and get present – this can be through a personal phone call, emails, text messages and face-to-face. Don't completely hand over your studio to your teachers. You need to ensure you have your fingers in all the pies, all the students know you and love you, as do the parents, and your teachers respect you.

Being a mentor to your teachers and managing their performance sets up an excellent foundation for building a solid teacher retention strategy. Teachers really are the backbone of your studio and you want to look after them. Sure, you're paying them to do a job but I've seen the biggest transformation in the teachers when my clients have implemented this retention strategy. This transformation doesn't just happen to the teachers – it ripples through the entire studio, which in turn boosts your bottom line.

Here are a few ideas to keep your teachers happy, hungry, honest and hard working!

Welcome To Our Studio
The first thing for us to talk about is how you welcome your teacher to the school. I'm sure you send them an email with all the details but you need to give them something tangible to take away after their first class. How about building up the hype with your students and parents that a new teacher is starting!

Get To Know Them
You'll want to get some personal information from the teacher that you can share through social media or through your newsletter promoting them. There are stacks of benefits to this, the main one being that it will get the parents and students talking about the exciting new teacher.

In the questions you'll send the teacher, you can include things like:

- Where did you grow up?
- Why do you love teaching dance?
- What can students expect from your classes?
- Who do you look up to? Who's your role model?
- Why are you excited to be teaching at Jazz Hands Dance Studio?

It's really that simple. They will send back some answers and then you can drip feed them across social media with the teacher's headshot for a few weeks and include the entire Q&A in the newsletter and your blog on your website before they start.

A Small Gift – Join Our Family
In terms of what you can give them after their first class, many of my studios have loved and implemented the idea of having one of their studio jackets created and printed with the teacher's name on it. You place this in a nice box with tissue paper, ribbon and a handwritten card from you outlining how grateful and excited you are for them to be joining the team. It's always wonderful seeing their face light up and the cost to put it together is nothing compared to the return you're going to get!

Your Team Retreat

My next retention strategy is to get out of the studio two or three times a year and have what I like to call Team Retreat. Maybe take them to a beachside location or somewhere in the mountains. During this day you may have an inspiring guest speaker to give them that little boost, share some food together and then get them involved in your business.

Get A Bit Social

Does your studio do social gatherings like dinners or go to the theatre as a group outside of dancing hours? Aside from the team retreats I encourage all of my clients to arrange at least three social gatherings for you and the teachers. This could be a dinner or going to the theatre. Now, I'm not saying you pay for this. Some studios I work with pay and some don't. Either way, it's not the cost that will count, it's the thought. These types of events are great to get out and simply relax and mingle with each other in a social setting. Some teachers may not know other teachers so it's also perfect for building the team culture. It's also an opportunity for you to say thank you and for your teachers to feel more than appreciated!

A big must-do is to have a calendar with all of your teachers' birthdays on it. You can do this online or simply create a document that gets updated every time you have a new teacher join. We've already gone through what to do when the new teacher joins. So for their birthday it's nice if you or your office staff can arrange a small gift and a card that the students can sign and give to their teacher in class. Your teacher will feel beyond loved – and make sure you get a group photo for Facebook and Instagram and tag everyone.

We've gone through a whole bunch of effective strategies in this chapter for how you recruit amazing teachers that stay. Take some time to go through this chapter a few times then start putting in place strategies and systems to bring in and grow your faculty.

Chapter Six

BUILDING YOUR LOCALLY FAMOUS STUDIO BRAND

'A brand is the set of expectations, memories, stories and relationships that, taken together, account for a consumer's decision to choose one product or service over another.' ~ Seth Godin

What do you think of when I say brand? Do you automatically think of Apple™ or Coca Cola?™ Or maybe you get a bit confused and ask yourself, 'What actually is a brand?' And what's the difference between branding and marketing?

I like to think of branding as the pull and marketing more as the push. Your studio brand is your truth and what you stand for, which communicates your values, attributes and characteristics. Quite simply, it's your promise to your customer – in your case, the customer being the student and parent.

Don't get me wrong, branding and marketing are certainly buddies! Your brand can encourage someone to enroll in your classes, but it doesn't say 'enroll today' like your marketing material would. Instead, it says, 'This is who we are. If you get a good feeling about us then explore a little more…' That's when the marketing kicks in.

What I love most about building a solid brand is that even once your marketing has come and gone, your brand still remains. Now for some, that's a good thing and others not, hence why you always need to be aware of the reputation you're building for the studio.

So how does your brand become a brand and how do your ideal students and parents connect with it? Well, they would first see or come across your brand through your logo and/or tagline. This could be on a piece of marketing, as they drive past your studio and see the signs or visit your website.

So what is your brand currently saying about your studio? Is it saying what you want it to say? More importantly, do you know what your studio stands for? Do you know the values and attributes your studio stands by, lesson after lesson?

To start building your brand, you need to ask yourself four questions:

1. What is your studio's mission?
It could provide tailored ballet programs for two to five-year-olds that enhances their creativity, social skills and happiness.

2. What are the benefits and features of your services?
Do this for all the services you offer at the studio, with classes being your main one. What do your students and parents already think of your studio? Ask around or send out a survey asking them what three words come to mind when they think of your studio.

3. What qualities do you want them to associate with your company?
Think about the values and attributes you want your studio to be known for and make a list of them.

Once you have dug deep to come up with your answers, you then need to follow these four steps.

1. Create a tagline – You would have heard hundreds of taglines over the years. Some examples you would know include:

- American Express - Don't leave home without it
- BMW - Sheer driving pleasure
- Nike - Just Do It
- Energizer Batteries - It keeps going, and going, and going
- Gillette - The best a man can get

2. Create a logo – Don't spend too much time on this or ask too many people what they think. Jump onto either Fiverr, Upwork or 99 Designs and you can outsource.

3. Create your core brand messages – These need to include a mix of your core values and attributes. You want to start each of your five core brand messages with 'A commitment to... .' So one might be 'A commitment to high quality dance training.'

4. Integrate your brand – Your brand needs to filter through from you answering the phone, responding to emails, presentation at competitions to your concert or recital experience.

MAKE A SPLASH WITH BRANDED CLASSES

Once you have built your brand foundation, it's time to start exploring how you can build mini brands around your classes. It's getting harder and harder to stand out from all the other jazz or ballet classes out there, so creating a brand around your classes is a great idea to excite your ideal students and parents quickly and really shine from the rest.

To give you an example, you may currently offer a jazz class for 6-8 year olds and you call it Jazz level 1 or Junior Jazz. The problem here is that every studio in your area has jazz classes for this age group, so what makes your classes different?

This is the exciting bit because you can create a sub brand for your dance studio that specifically targets this age group and makes you stand out from the crowd. Most studios that I work with have already created a mini syllabus of sorts that they teach this age group, so why not give your own program an awesome name?! For example, Groovy Groovers (that's what we had!). Create something unique so that you can really zoom in on these parents and deliver them a targeted message with your marketing. This strategy doesn't just apply to your younger classes. You may have a musical theatre class that you run weekly for teenagers – instead of calling it Teenage Musical Theatre, you might call it Showbiz Stars or Musical Madness. Simply by creating a few branded classes for age groups outside of your different levels and exam work, you can generate more interest and buzz in your offering as well as becoming the 'go to' studio that doesn't just run your average dance class, but offers tailored and structured programs.

So what are the steps you need to take to create a branded class?

1. Identify the age group – Go through the classes you offer and identify age groups and styles that has either:

a) been strong in the past but dropped off recently, or
b) has increased recently but still has loads of potential.

2. Create names – Get your whole team involved and come up with names for the classes. Some studio owners run a competition in the studio where the parents and students put in their ideas and the person who comes up with the name you select wins a prize.

3. Get a logo – Jump online and have a logo made up for the new class.

That's it! Three easy steps to creating a branded class at your studio, which has only cost you the price of the logos.

MAKE YOUR BRAND COME ALIVE THROUGH YOUR WEBSITE

Once you have a solid brand in place, it's time to ensure your website is doing the best job it can – and that's bringing you in more new students.

This is the latest in what's working to generate leads, build your list and get people to take action with the outcome of them or their child becoming a student. I speak with studio owners every day, so you can imagine how many dance studio websites I'm looking at. It pains me to say it, but there are so many poor websites out there, and it blows my mind that some dance studios don't even have websites. There's really no excuse, as we're now a part of a global market place, meaning you don't need to spend thousands of dollars on a website, you can outsource the job and get great results for a fraction of what it used to cost back when I had an agency build my first website for $25,000! Crazy, right?!

The biggest mistake I see studio owners make with their website is that they create it for their existing dance families, when your website should be aimed at new potential students. The objective is to bring in and collect the contact details of these potential new students, but instead websites are cluttered with recital or concert information, student announcements, overdue fee notices and more information that a new parent or student doesn't need to read – information that just distracts them or leaves them overwhelmed, therefore unlikely to even reach out and enquire.

3 COMMON WEBSITE MISTAKES

When it comes to websites, there are three common mistakes that studio owners make when putting one together and I want to share them with you now.

1. They do it themselves – It makes no sense to me why a studio owner would build their own website. By the time you watch the tutorials, do all the design, development and uploading, you would have spent at least 50 hours (and a few tears, I'm sure!) and you won't get the same sleek looking and efficiently functioning site as you would with someone who makes websites for a living. We're extremely lucky that websites don't need to cost us an arm and a leg. You certainly pay for what you get, but I've had one client recently who had their website designed and developed for $350USD. Sure, there are no bells or whistles, but it definitely does the job. I've had other client who spent around $2,000 for awesome websites. It all depends on your requirements and where you get the site created – in your country or overseas.

2. There is no IFG! So you probably want to know what an IFG is... well, it's your number one lead generating magnet. It's your irresistible free gift, which I'm going to dig deep into shortly. This is a tool or offer you're going to give away on your website. For example, a free unlimited one-week class pass where they give you their contact details in return for the class pass.

3. Too much information. It's a sad fact, but people don't read every page of your website. The content on your website needs to be clear and to the point with strong calls to action. A call to action is simply a line such as 'Call us today on 123 456 789 to register for your free one-week unlimited class pass.'

Okay, so you're ready to either create your website or renovate your current website. Here's what you need to start thinking of.

Design – As a creative, I'm sure you have a bunch of ideas for how you want your website to look. But for a moment, I want you to take a step back and put yourself in the shoes of a parent or student who will be coming to your website, and start thinking about what they want to see. Spend a few hours on the internet and start looking for eye-catching, simple yet effective design – surf the net and come up with a list of five websites that you love the design of that you think will capture your ideal students and parents. By the way, these can be from any industry, not just dance. In fact, I'd prefer you to look outside of the industry at other services-based business' sites. You then want to continue your search and seek out five websites that have excellent, easy-to-use navigation and that have created a really intuitive user experience. What we want to look out for here is a site that has FLOW. There's no clutter, it gives you straight to the point, useful information and you feel like it leads you through a journey on the site.

Once you have these 10 sites listed (some may cross over) you'll start to form a picture in your head of what your website should look like and how your audience will experience it. These are crucial elements to get on before you move forward.

Before we move on and look at your website layout, I wanted to share with you some invaluable advice I received from one of my mentors, *Book Yourself Solid* author, Michael Port. Michael says that when it comes to your website, there are three questions you need to ask yourself for each page:

1. Who is coming here? – Generally, this will be your ideal student or parent avatar. See if the page you have has been created for them in its design, imagery and content.

2. What do I want them to do? – Every single page should have an objective. When they click on a specific page on your website, what is your objective for that page? Is it for them to call you to book in for a class? Is it for them to register for a trial? Whatever the objective, ensure you have one for each.

3. How am I going to get them to do it? – This is about things like page layout, use of colours. There is a great website called whichtestwon.com and it shows you results from split testing; which page layouts and calls to action out-performed another. I'm a bit of a tech nerd when it comes to these things, so I love this site. This will help you when deciding placement of your calls to action and opt in offers.

Okay, so let's have a look at your website layout. I want to go through a format that I use with our program members that has them generating more leads, while giving their audience relevant information to take the appropriate action.

Your top navigation is where all the page headlines sit for your website. Let's have a look at an effective top navigation formula for your studio's website.

ABOUT

Our Journey – Include your values and mission in this page. When you're writing this, ensure that you're speaking to your ideal student and telling a story.

Our Teachers – Make it personal and professional. Tell us who their favorite artist is or what's their coffee order etc. Your teachers are the role models of your studio. It would also be greatly beneficial to have a short 30 sec-1 min video of each of your teachers introducing themselves and saying hello.

Love Letters (testimonials) – Have a whole page of testimonials with photos and phone numbers. Reach out to your parents, senior students and graduates for their personal thoughts on the studio.

We Answer Your Questions (videos or written) – Pick 5-10 questions that are regularly asked by new enquiries that come through and either film a quick 1-2 minute video or have a written answer.

CLASSES

Our Classes - There are a few ways you can explain classes, but whichever way you choose, you don't just want to give a description of what jazz or tap is. You want to let them know what that style means to you, your teachers and how you teach it at your studio. You can convey this through an image with text, or you can have a short 20-30 sec video where you explain the style while cutting in to video clips of that style (maybe from class, competitions or your concert or recital).

HOW TO JOIN US

This should be a simple step-by-step process of how a new student can join your studio. No crazy long rules and policies here, just an easy to follow process that gets people through the door.

You will see that I don't have the timetable mentioned on here. Over the years, I've been experimenting with my private clients having and not having the timetable on the website, and what we've found is that by having a timetable, a parent or student will look at what they think is their correct class and then go, 'Oh no, can't make that...' and won't enquire. You want to give them every opportunity to reach out to you to gain more information so that they can either speak with someone on the phone or through email. It's important that you get the opportunity to speak with them before they self-eliminate and you don't get the enquiry. There is a page that has your timetable on it in your website, but it's a hidden page and you give the link to students and their parents once they join.

NEWS

This is your blog with the latest news that should be updated weekly. You can write an article, something on competition results, preparing for exams, guest teachers, workshops, summer camps and the list goes on. Have some written pieces plus images and video if you can. Update this on the same time each week for consistency.

CONTACT

Simply have a regular contact form that will get sent straight through to your studio's email address. You may also include phone numbers on this contact page.

Once you have these elements in place, it's time for you to create a homepage that is engaging, informative (not too much information) and caters to your different ideal students and parents. Use the elements we have mentioned above – include photos and videos.

Chapter Seven

EVERGREEN STUDENT ENROLLMENT BLUEPRINT

'We see our customers as invited guests to a party, and we are the hosts. It's our job to make the customer experience a little bit better.' ~ Jeff Bezos, Amazon.com

Before we tackle your new student enrollment process, we need to identify who your ideal students are… the students, and parents, who see what you're offering and think, 'Yes, that's exactly what I've been looking for!'

The biggest mistake I see with studio owners who come to me for help is that they haven't clearly defined who their ideal student is, and we all know that we can't be all things to all people, right? We just end up chasing our tail and don't have consistent new enrollments, which means our bank balance suffers and people come through the door who you don't want (poor payers, high maintenance parents etc.).

When you have clarity on your ideal students for specific classes, you can create a super targeted marketing and engagement plan with messaging that's extremely relevant for them – which will increase your leads and overall conversion rate of new students.

As a studio owner, there are three main things you need to consider when creating your ideal student profile:

1. Student
2. Class
3. Parent

The first, of course, is the student. You then need to decide which classes the ideal student would fit into, and last but not least, create a mini avatar for your ideal student's parent. As we know, a five-year-old is not taking themself off to dance class, so we need to focus our marketing on their parents or grandparents.

GAIN CLARITY ON YOUR IDEAL STUDENT

When you combine all three components, you gain real clarity on who it is you're actually marketing to. This affects how you market to your ideal student, from imagery, copy, the language you use and how you're actually getting your message to them, whether it be via online or offline marketing strategies.

Ideal Student + Class = Relevance

When you partner your ideal student with the appropriate classes, you create relevance and this is crucial for boosting your leads and conversion rate. You want to ensure that the student you're targeting sees an advert or receives a piece of marketing and says, 'I want to try that!'

Class + Parent = Value

When you group the relevant class with your ideal student's parent, you create value. A parent will recognize the relevance and then support their child in their decision to start taking a class or classes with you.

Student + Parent = Commitment

Finally, when the student and the parent are on the same page, you create commitment. Again, commitment from the student and the parent is crucial to help both parties when exploring what becoming a student with your studio would be like.

Ideal Student

So let's break this down a little bit for you. When I talk about creating your ideal student avatar, this is what you'll explore:

- Age
- Gender
- Where they live
- What school they go to and their year level

- Interests and other hobbies
- Dreams – Why are they coming to your studio? Fitness, social, professional
- Fears – What's stopping them? Parental support, finances, bullying, lack of time

Class

- Style of dance (jazz, tap, ballet, hip hop)
- Level or Stream (you may have a fun stream and a performance stream)

Parent

- Age range
- Gender
- Relationship status
- Occupation
- Salary
- Hobbies and other interests
- Dream for their child – to be a professional performer
- Fears – why not support their child? Low in funds, no time, can't see the value in dance

This is a great place for you to start your journey to becoming the 'go to' studio in your area; by building your ideal student profiles, you will have a few of these depending on what you offer at your studio. It doesn't matter where you are in your studio's journey, whether you're starting up the business or you've been in business for years, it's never too early or too late to get clear on who it is you want to attract into your studio.

Can you see how your entire business can change, just by gaining absolute clarity on the students you want in your studio? You'll receive better results from your marketing as it will be very targeted and relevant, you'll be attracting the right type of students and parents to your studio which means your retention rates will increase, teachers will be happier, parents and students will be happier... which, as a bonus, will increase your referrals. And all of the above will make you, the business owner, happier. This is the first step to creating targeted marketing and engagement campaigns that actually work.

YOUR STUDENT ENROLLMENT PROCESS

Now that you know who you want to attract to your studio, let me show you how you can build your new student enrollments through my proven blueprint. Hundreds of Dance Studio Owners in our programs have used this exact formula to generate big results when it comes to filling up their classes, and I'm glad that you'll now have this tool too!

I want you to think about your current enrollment process for a minute. When a potential student or parent sends you an email or calls, what process do you have in place to have them or their child become a student?

It's important that you have your enrollment process set in concrete. This goes beyond just getting someone in for a trial and signing them up. I've developed this 11-step enrollment process that ensures you're not losing students through the gaps.

Many Studio Owners have new enquiries coming through the door, but they see them once and they never come again, or they book a trial and never turn up. You must put a solid enrollment process in place immediately!

But I'm taking the guesswork out of this process for you from this day forward!

11 STEPS CHECKLIST TO ENROLL NEW STUDENTS

Step 1 – Take The Enquiry & Book Trial Or Class

As soon as you receive an email or phone enquiry, you want to thank the parent and student and give them details on how they can book into their trial class (or similar). This is also a good opportunity to build some credibility – basically explain why your dance studio is the place for them. IMPORTANT: This conversation needs to be about what the potential student wants, not about how amazing your studio is (listening is key).

Step 2 – Email Trial Class Confirmation

As soon as you or your office staff book the new student into the class, be sure you send a confirmation email to the parent or student with everything they need to know, along with some of your commonly asked questions so they know exactly what to expect when they arrive (no surprises!). Also mention to come in 15 minutes early so you can explain more about the studio and answer any of their questions (this is where you will do the pre-class consults – more on that in Step 4). Add their contact details to your potential student database (for future marketing campaigns).

Step 3 – 24 Hour 'See You Soon' SMS

24 hours before their trial class, you should send an SMS with the class details, address, phone number and have them text you back Y to confirm or call you to re-schedule. This is a hugely important piece of the enrollment process. If they are not coming you will want to know and, more importantly, you will want to re-schedule them for the next available class.

Step 4 – Pre-Class Consult

This is my 'secret sauce' step. You or your office person will be expecting the family for their class, so make sure you already know their name and greet them warmly when they come into the studio. You then want to have what I like to call the 'pre-class consult' – this is about a 15-minute conversation with the family where you can assess their needs and provide them with more information about why your studio is a great fit for them.

Step 5 – Introduction To The Teacher & Class Buddy

Walk the student into class and introduce them to the teacher, then have the teacher introduce them to a buddy for the class. Your teacher should have about 3-5 buddies that they call upon regularly to look after students trialling your studio. This instantly calms the student down and eliminates any chance of them feeling like an outsider. When selecting your buddies, you want to ensure it's the happy, passionate and fun student – not the super competitive 'I need to be front and center' student.

Step 6 – Homework – Stick Strategy

In the last five minutes of class, have the teacher leave the students with something to work on for next week. It may be to practice a combination they learned in groups that they will present at the start of class next week, or maybe it's learning a song for next week's musical theatre class.

Step 7 – After Class Follow Up

This is where I see too many studio owners drop the ball and let the student and parent leave without asking for the enrollment. Have a conversation about how things went in class and ask them to enroll. Ideally, they have tried a few classes that day and you can simply ask, 'So, what shall we get you enrolled in… both the jazz and tap classes?' Don't be afraid to make the sale happen.

What's Next?

By following this process you should be getting around 70-80% of people enrolling. At this point, you then move them into your onboarding process (how to retain students). If they need to think about it and don't enroll on that day, go to Step 8!

Step 8 – 24-Hour Call

At the end of their time at your studio, you would have let them know that you or your office staff will be in touch over the next day to answer any of their questions. You give them a call between 24-48 hours (no more than 48) and check in to see where they are at. At this point, you may want to offer an incentive like 50% of the enrollment fee or something similar. The idea is that you encourage them to put all their cards on the table so you can answer any objections and know where they stand. Important: Make sure your offer has an expiry date!

Step 9 – 4 Days Later Email

Send an email after four days simply stating your offer to them again, letting them know it's expiring and that you would love to see them join your dance studio family. Make this personal and speak directly to them. You could also record a quick personal video to send to them – this has been effective for many of our Studio Success Formula program members.

Step 10 – 7 Days Later Phone Call

This is your last shot for now. Call the parent or student and check in with them. Let them know that you appreciate that life is busy, but you just wanted to check in and see if they had made a decision about enrolling in your studio. If their answer is not now (never treat a 'no' as never), then add them to your 'trialled but not enrolled' database so you can continue to keep in touch and stay top of their mind.

Step 11 – Keep In Touch

Be sure you send them an email within the next 30 days. It could be a newsletter, birthday email, class offer or similar, but remember that them saying 'no' doesn't mean it will be a no forever. Besides, keeping top of mind means you may even receive referrals from them!

Right now, I know you're thinking one of two things:

1. No way Clint, that's too pushy.
2. This is awesome! No wonder we haven't been enrolling as many students as we'd like.

If you're totally on board with thought number two, then I'm pumped for you to start implementing this process today!

On the other hand, if you're in the thought number one camp, I want to ask you a question… do you have the best training in your area? Do you have awesome, passionate and experienced teachers? Do you care more than anything about creating an environment for students that not only makes them better dancers but better human beings?

If you said yes to all of these, then by not following an enrollment process, you're essentially not giving your potential new families all the information they need to make the right decision for them.

Chances are if you're not enrolling this student who has shown interest in dance, someone else in your area is. I'm sure you'd like that to be you because of the great service you provide, so please, at least try implementing this process.

It's worked for hundreds of studio owners around the world and I'd love to add you to that list as well! Start implementing this process today and start to see the difference it makes over the coming week.

Chapter Eight
ATTRACT IDEAL STUDENTS WITH DIGITAL MARKETING

'The aim of marketing is to get customers to know, like and trust you.' ~ Unknown

I first fell in love with marketing when I didn't even know it was called that. In the first year of owning my dance studio, I used to come up with ways to bring new students in the door and design the artwork – mostly newspaper adverts and flyers back in those days. I then went on to study marketing and became obsessed with it during my five years working as a Senior Celebrity Agent at the Harry M Miller Group in Sydney, Australia. I'm also slightly obsessed with how a business or business owner goes from being undiscovered to an authority. Over my five years as an agent, and then creating and selling my three businesses (including a dance studio), I've been able to create a formula for becoming an authority – and today I'm going to share with you the online strategies that you can implement into your studio's marketing plan to become the 'go to' studio.

STUMPED BY SOCIAL MEDIA?

Hands up if social media confuses you? I get you, I really do, but news on the street is that social media is not going anywhere, fast... which means if you haven't already embraced it, it's about time you took the plunge.

I'm going to hold your hand and walk you through my simple social media strategy. You don't need to have any prior knowledge as this is a paint by numbers section of the chapter, to ensure you get clarity and a great understanding of how it works, but more importantly, why you're doing it!

Before you roll up your social media sleeves, we need to work out where you should be playing, and to do that, we need to know where your ideal students and their parents are spending the majority of their time. The saying 'You can't be all things to all people in your business' certainly applies to social media. You want to master one or two platforms instead of being spread across them all and none of them being effective!

Step one is about identifying where your students and parents are hanging out. Over many years of working with studio owners, I have discovered that most studios have Facebook as their primary platform, as students and parents are on Facebook, with Instagram or Pinterest as their secondary platform – Instagram drawing in the students and Pinterest attracting the mothers. And as I write this book, Snapchat is growing ever popular with the students as well.

Get Clear On Your Goals

So, once we have our platforms we need to discuss why we're posting on these platforms. What's our objective? This is one of the most important questions you should be asking yourself each time you implement a marketing strategy. You see, most studios think that Social Media is part of their student attraction strategy, but truth be told, creating solid social media platforms is about building awareness of your studio and boosting your retention. If someone gains awareness of your studio through seeing a post or a student shares something through social media, that's the first step. You then need to get them across to your website to opt in for your Irresistible Free Gift, or to contact the studio directly for more information.

So that's the objective – to connect with our current students and parents online to keep them engaged, informed and inspired around the clock. The action we want them to be taking is liking, sharing, commenting and clicking on the links within our posts.

What Can I Post?

The big question I always get asked, 'Clint, what things can I post on social media?' Let's go through all the types of content (20, to be exact!) that you can post across your social media accounts.

- Branded quotes
- Social photos – picnics, theatre, discos
- Photos from competitions and events
- Videos from class
- Photos from class
- Inspiring videos from YouTube/Vimeo
- Audio recordings – interviews with dancers
- Infographics
- Graphs
- SlideShare presentations
- Articles
- Blogs
- Podcasts
- Webinars
- Competitions
- Newsletters
- Press release
- Questions – get opinions
- Special offers
- Online video training

That will keep you busy! So now you have loads of options in terms of the content you can post, let's talk about the frequency and when to post.

When we talk about how often you should be posting on Facebook, it should be between 2-3 times per day. My advice would be to start with two and gauge how your audience reacts to it. In terms of the best times to post your content, this is something that will take some time to figure out, after trialling what works best for your business. There are many studies out there that discuss the best times which I've tested with my studio owner private clients, and at the end of the day, it's about working out what works best for your audience.

The great thing about social media is that all your posts can be scheduled at the one time, either using the scheduling tool that is part of that platform or using software like Post Planner, Hootsuite or Buffer. This means you can sit down for 30 minutes to an hour, once a week, and schedule it all in. Obviously, you want to still be able to save space for those great videos or pictures from class that you or your teachers can upload on the spot! Which touches on another great point – don't feel like you're the only person from your studio who can contribute to the page. Have some guidelines in place and trial some of your teachers having access to post something cool from class. I've seen this be highly effective, as after the class, the teacher says, 'Hey everyone, jump on Facebook or Instagram and like and share it with your friends.' This is gold, and you haven't even had to do anything!

When it comes to Instagram, you can post a lot of the content we have spoken about – photos, videos, quotes and this list goes on. Your students will love this. Have them tag your studio in their posts and they will basically populate this platform for you.

Facebook Advertising

Have you heard about this Facebook advertising craze that's going on? I'm sure you've been exposed through your Facebook account to adverts on all types of things. Who knows... maybe that's how you found out about this book!

If you haven't tried Facebook advertising, then it's time you learn... and learn quickly, before the price goes up and the effectiveness goes down.

I want to give you four steps to mastering your Facebook advertising campaigns because it's recently been such a popular topic of conversation between our program members. In the past six months, collectively we have spent more than $50,000 on Facebook advertising. With that kind of experience, I'm bringing you our latest learnings on what works and what doesn't.

First, let's talk about the biggest way studio owners are WASTING money on Facebook advertising — and that's by buying 'Likes'. Spending money on getting more likes on your studio's Facebook page results in your number of Facebook followers growing, but not your student numbers or revenue. Instead, you need to turn that ad spend into money spent more efficiently. You do that through targeted campaigns that result in new student enrollments.

Here are 4 steps to mastering Facebook advertising today:

1. Bull's-Eye Targeting

The studios that are blowing it out of the water are the ones creating super-targeted adverts. Potential dance parents and students want to see relevant advertisements, which means you need to step it up. It's time to stop doing the blanket advert that covers all ages and all styles: remember, when you talk to many, you talk to no one. Instead, you need to target multiple types of students and parents. For example, you might create an advert to enroll more preschool-age children. This would be very different from the advert that you'd create for your 8-10-year-old hip-hop class. The first step is to clearly define what age groups and styles you want to target. Get specific! Facebook allows you to target locations, so make sure you're not wasting money targeting an area that you know people won't travel to your studio from.

2. Perfect Match

Once you know exactly who your advert is targeting, ensure that your image and copy (text) are aligned. For example, if you want to fill adult jazz classes, use an image of an adult doing jazz. It might sound simple, but you'd be amazed at how many times I see a mismatch between the image and the target. You'll also want to look at the copy you're placing in the advert. If you're using the regular ads dashboard, you'll be limited in the amount of text you can place. The solution to this is to use Facebook's power editor, which gives you more freedom and flexibility in creating high-performing adverts. Your text is very important, so make sure you're speaking exactly to the person the advert was created for.

Tip: images can only contain up to 20% text.

3. Convert Like Crazy

With over 10 different types of Facebook advertising available, it can be difficult to know which one to select. Let's simplify by using an example:

say you want to gain new student enquiries. Most studio owners would do a clicks-to-website campaign, but I want you to go deeper by creating a campaign with the objective of website conversions. This means that when someone gives you their details for a free trial class or similar offer, Facebook will track that and count it as one conversion, which will then assign a price per conversion. This means you know exactly how much it's costing you for a new student lead. You can set this up in the power editor.

4. Test & Measure

The most important step in Facebook advertising is to test and measure. There's no magic pill when it comes to figuring out what's going to knock it out of the park for you, which is why you need to test (with a small budget), look at the results and then decide whether to scale your advert up or down. After 24 hours, check the advert to see what your conversions are costing; then, after two days, decide whether to adjust it or leave it. To take testing and measuring to the next level, start split-testing the adverts by changing the image or text to see which version performs best.

Facebook advertising is something that takes time to understand, so please be patient. It's not going away any time soon, so it's crucial you learn their advertising platform to help grow your dance studio. I've seen it work for studios in small country towns to large cities across the world.

Social media isn't the only online platform to get your message out there and secure new student enrollments. Let me run you through the remaining effective ways you can market your studio online.

NEWSLETTER

Your newsletter is one of the most effective communication tools to speak with your current dance families, as well as potential new families and families who have left. Did you see here that I mentioned two target groups?

Let's start by talking about your newsletter for the families currently at your studio. This should be a great mix of sharing big news (student achievements, competition results etc), upcoming events at the studio and keeping them in the know. Overall this is an upbeat newsletter – even give it a name like the Studio Name Times or something similar.

You could even run a competition at your studio for them to name the name of your newsletter. This newsletter has two objectives… to inform and to retain. Give them the information they need and tell them about all the great things that are happening at your studio.

Now, the other newsletter I mentioned is one that goes to potential customers and old customers. You should also send this out once a month, and this newsletter should use the same upbeat and proud content that you have in your studio newsletter. You'll need to take out studio specific details and add a strong call to action in it about starting class. You can lead them to your IFG – unlimited class pass or have them call the studio directly. People from this list will unsubscribe, which is fine. The whole idea around this is staying top of mind. It might not be them who ends up coming to class, but they could refer your studio to a friend or family member.

EMAIL MARKETING

This is one of the most effective ways to get people to take action. The result, though, is based on how relevant the message is to the audience and how effective you use language in the email. Email marketing is used in the broader business world to accelerate the pace in which you grow a relationship (build trust and credibility), that is then usually followed with an invitation for you to buy something. As an example, let's say you have a new uniform that you're launching at the studio. To get the most exposure for the launch of the new range, you could send a number of emails over seven days that walks them through the process of you creating, designing and making the new uniforms. It's all about story-telling, and making your customers feel like they're a part the process will leave them wanting to grab the new uniforms as soon as they're ready. This strategy can be applied to anything… concert or recital tickets, summer camps and workshops, product launches. You can also back this campaign up by including content on Facebook and Instagram to generate greater coverage.

WRITE BLOGS OR ARTICLES

On the news section of your website, you should have news about what's happening at your studio plus some articles from you or your teachers about things that could add massive value to your families and potential new families. Now, when I talk about writing, I don't want you to freak out because you don't need to be an excellent writer to publish blogs and articles. There are excellent copywriters out there who can take your idea from a few dot points or sentences and turn them into an interesting, digestable 250-500 word article.

Once you have written an article, it's important you push it out to as many people as possible. Share it on your newsletter, through social media and also through article directories like Ezinearticles. This will basically syndicate your articles to other websites, which will increase the coverage plus boost your search engine optimization.

WRITE GUEST BLOGS OR ARTICLES

Identify dance-related blogs or websites where your ideal students are looking and post some articles there. Some of them may allow you to post the same articles you've written for your website on their site, or they might need to be exclusive. The exposure for writing on other sites is awesome, plus it really boosts your credibility. Just be careful of one thing – you want to ensure the website has great traffic being generated to the site and your article. There is no point spending the time writing articles for websites that have a small amount of visitors. You also want to make sure they'll push your article out through social media and their newsletter if they have one. So, how to start here is to make a list of 10 or so websites or blogs that you know are popular and put together a pitch letter for them that outlines why you should write for them. If you're unsure of the blogs and websites out there, ask your students what they're reading or looking at which will give you a great indication!

WRITE A GUIDE

This is certainly the era of content marketing. Content marketing simply means giving away massive value for free to your ideal customer in the form of a guide, e-book, video training, audio series. I want you to think about something that you could have on your website to give away – similar to what you could have for your IFG, but give it away for free, such as a direct download. You could create a guide that is… *The 8 Things All Professional Dancers Have In Common* or *6 Interviews With World Class Choreographers on what they look for when hiring a dancer.* To make this happen, simply have a phone conversation with six choreographers, then have it transcribed on Fiverr or post a job up on Upwork. Next, have a graphic designer put it into a well-designed PDF. You can then promote it on your website, social media... anywhere, really. This is an excellent way for you to position yourself and your studio (as you will include your contact details in the guide along with your studio name) as the 'go to' person for dance in your area. It's awesome and doesn't take too much time. The great thing is that once you create it, you can continually promote it. Create once and use it for years!

GOOGLE PLACES & MAPS

This is a very simple way to be found on Google – just google Google Places, follow the prompts and your business listing will be live in no time at no cost. The other benefit is that it will also help you greatly with Search Engine Optimization.

ONLINE DIRECTORIES

Depending on where you are in the world, there will be a number of directories that would be beneficial for you to list your business in to help more people find you – and help boost your overall ranking with Google. There are new directories launching all the time, so just do some research on Google and start adding your listing straight away!

ADWORDS

You may have heard of AdWords or 'pay per click' advertising. AdWords is how Google search generates their revenue and I'm sure you would have seen many examples of Google ads when you've been surfing the net. AdWords is a platform that allows you to bid on certain search words or terms so that when someone searches for, for example, Dance Studio Brooklyn, you can create an advert and bid on this search term so that you'll come up when the search happens. This is a very simple way of explaining quite a complicated concept.

REMARKETING

A more advanced strategy you may want to implement is remarketing, which is also part of the options available in Adwords and Facebook advertising. Remarketing is a very cool strategy, and one you've probably seen in action. You know when you're visiting a website, you're about to buy something and you decide now is the right time... and then you get distracted and forget about it. Then, like magic, the product or website shows up in an advert on another website or on your Facebook page.

Well, this isn't magic – this is remarketing. Basically, AdWords and Facebook will give you, or your web developer, coding to put into a page on your website. Then every time someone leaves that page, Google and Facebook follows them and serves them adverts while they browse the net. Pretty amazing, right? Not only is it great for getting new student leads in the door, it's also great for building awareness and increasing retention. Imagine someone goes to sign up for your unlimited 7-day class pass, but doesn't end up signing up because they got distracted or felt a bit of fear at the last minute… you can them serve them with banner or text adverts across the Google network (even YouTube) or Facebook and Instagram that reminds them to get their pass. It's truly amazing and highly cost effective.

GROUP BUYING DEALS

Warning: this strategy is a little controversial! Some studios have been burned in the past by using group buying sites because they come for two weeks, do the classes and never come back. In saying that, some studio owners have had great success with group buying deals because they have a solid enrollment and lead-nurturing process in place. Group buying deals are not suitable for all dance studios – you need to have capacity to take a large number of new students and generally be in a location close to a main city (again, dependent on the country you're in). Some of my larger studio private mentoring clients will introduce new classes just for the group buying campaigns, knowing that they won't all become regular students – so instead of disrupting current classes, they operate separate ones and if they want to stay, only then put them into the normal classes. Some ideas, in terms of offers, that we have used in the past include 10 classes in 10 days. It doesn't need to be one a day, as you might not have enough classes for that age group. Another idea is to offer two weeks of classes. The important thing with these offers is to make sure you look after these leads from the moment they step in the door to the moment they leave each class.

MOBILE APP ADVERTISING

Local coffee mobile app advertising is a new territory for dance studio owners, but one that will become very big in the coming years. I won't spend too much time on this, as there are not an abundance of opportunities here, although one campaign I've seen work very well is with the local coffee shops or cafes that use a coffee app. There are quite a few coffee stores that use apps where their customers order their coffee on the app and it's ready when they arrive. As this advertising medium is quite new, it's inexpensive and when you think about targeting local parents in the area, it's a great way to get more visibility for your studio. From the app you would have a banner or full screen advert that would take them to your opt-in page for the unlimited class pass. It's definitely worth looking into with your local coffee shops and cafes.

VIDEO MARKETING

Video is a fantastic way to promote your studio. With any video you take you need to be ensuring that it's uploaded to your YouTube channel, and if I can give you a small tip for this, it would be to make sure you put your website in the description right up the top and the address of your studio in under the description of the video. This is going to give you more click throughs to your website! Other ideas for video you might showcase on YouTube are showreels of the studio (a day in the life), guest teacher workshop snippets, videos from behind the scenes at competitions... the list goes on. You can also share these videos on social media, your blogs and newsletters once you've uploaded them to YouTube. Just make sure that you have written permission from the parents and students that you can take photos and video footage of them.

As you can see from the diverse online ways you can market your business, there is no reason you can't be enrolling new students each week into your studio. It's about getting clear on your goals, which you did in Chapter 1, and then putting in place your action plan to ensure you reach them. These marketing strategies are going to get you to those goals faster!

Chapter Nine

OFFLINE MARKETING THAT CONNECTS AND CONVERTS

'Marketing is really just about sharing your passion.'
~ Michael Hyatt

I remember when I had my studio about 13 years ago, you could easily generate a large number of new leads through a newspaper advert. Do you remember those days? There would be an opportunity for you to have a print advertisement in a performing arts or dance feature with the other studios, and this is how people did their marketing.

But that was then. These days, newspaper adverts, flyers in the postbox and print directory adverts are dying fast, yet there are still studios out there using these mediums because they don't know what else to do. You now have the digital strategies to incorporate from the last chapter, but we must not forget about offline marketing. When we go offline with our marketing, that's where we truly get the opportunity to stand out from the pack!

Although these are offline marketing strategies, the idea here is that you're driving traffic to a dedicated webpage where your potential student or parent only have one option – to register for your offer, whether it be a free class, a free week of classes, a class and some merchandise... there are many opportunities. We've already talked about your offer, so hopefully you have decided what yours is.

Let's go through a number of ways you can promote your studio through imagery and language, then we can apply these strategies to a number of different offline advertising mediums.

Here are the 4 elements that make for an effective advert:

1. It connects with the audience
2. It's memorable and easy to recall
3. It doesn't confuse the viewer or make them hunt for information
4. It provides information quickly and succinctly

So now we know what makes for an effective ad, what do we need to include in our advert to tick all these boxes?

PRINT ADVERTISING

There are 6 things that every print advert must have. These are:

1. Logo – This is what your studio is known for. It doesn't need to take up the majority of the space – just being on the page will allow people to identify that this is your studio.

2. Headline – This needs to be larger than the rest of your text on the advert and you want it to grab attention!

3. Tagline – This is where you can give the audience the benefit of coming to your studio or why your studio is unique.

4. Image – Use an image that your target age group will identify with.

5. Testimonial – Have a short sentence from a current student.

6. Call To Action – Call us today on… or visit (website address). The important thing here is that if you're taking them to a website, it needs to be extremely relevant to the advert, and allows them to give you their details to receive your free trial class or unlimited 7-day pass. Don't take them to your homepage as they'll end up losing their way.

I also wanted to share with you a few other tips for creating an effective print advert:

Less is more: Don't try and place everything that your business does on one advert. Give them what they need to know, have a clear and bold call to action that drives them to take immediate action, and you're done. Consumers are being bombarded with around 625 adverts per day – that's a lot of clutter to get through. Make your ad clear and direct, so that it makes it to the top of that clutter pile.

White space is good: Don't feel like you need to fill each space in the advert. White space can be quite effective in that it makes your ad stand out more so than if you were to fill every inch with text and images. Think about how you feel as a reader; you want clean, neat designs and just enough words to give you the information you're after.

Top to bottom: Look at how you'll stack your advert. Use a mixture of text sizes. For instance, your headline would be larger than your tagline. Your image may be the focal point of the advert with smaller text. Look at your proportions and test how appealing it is to the eye.

Colour combinations: By always going with a light background with darker text, your advert is going to be easier to read. Studies over the years have shown that if you follow this format, your conversion rate will increase.

Proof it: Grab two people who are not part of the project to proofread your advert. There's nothing worse than seeing a typo in a piece of marketing. Nothing.

Now, let's look at the avenues you can explore to get your dance studio out there offline, using printed materials.

Letter Box Flyers

This is one of those advertising mediums that used to be highly effective, but over the years the leads from using this method has dropped significantly. There is still hope, though – recently I did a number of these campaigns with my private clients who followed the format we just discussed and they got excellent results! Let me explain to you why:

With a letterbox drop, you can select the areas you want to target with the company you use or maybe you'll gather a group of students and parents to do it with you on the weekend. Firstly, what I like to do is work out where your current students live. Get your enrollment forms or online records and work out the top five suburbs your students are coming from – this saves you targeting areas that may not be interested in dance classes. You also have the ability to test new suburbs by only testing a street or two as a sample to see whether or not it's worthwhile doing the rest of the area. Testing is so important in all of your marketing and to be honest, it's the one thing I don't see happening enough with studio owners. With the right advert and right area, a flyer drop can be extremely effective. Ideally, and if you have the budget, you would run your flyer campaign to the same houses twice within a month-long period to increase your brand awareness, which would give them a better chance of taking action.

There are a number of other places you can hand out flyers, including at the train and subway stations, which are close to your studio for the mums and dads heading to work or arriving home.

Setting Up A Stall

Setting up a stall or table at a local mall or shopping centre is another way to generate awareness of your studio. You can generate a lot of leads simply by setting up a great looking table with a TV playing a DVD of your last concert or recital, some pull up banners and possibly balloons to make it a little more appealing to the eye. On the day you can sign up new students for your 7-day unlimited class pass by booking them in to start next week. You'll also send them a confirmation email within 24 hours to confirm the details. Also, you can run a competition to win a month's worth of classes. You'll collect their name, number, age and email address, then you can call all the people who didn't win and invite them in anyway for seven days of classes for free. This is a great way to build your lead database. The key here is to make sure you follow up with your leads within 48 hours.

Car Advertising

Do you have a car? If you do, is it branded? Car branding is an extremely effective way to promote your studio, especially if you do quite a bit of driving around your local area. You may also be able to park your car out the front of your studio to drive additional promotion. The most important thing is to ensure you have an offer; you either want people to call you directly for their trial class or similar. In line with this you can create bumper stickers for your family that says, 'We're part of the XYZ Studio Family. Join the fun!' with your website address. I've seen this work extremely well. Some studio owners incentivize their families by giving them one week of classes for free if they take a photo of the sticker with the car and tag the studio in a Facebook post. You'd be surprised how many people jump on board!

Studio Signage

Some studio owners have better locations than others when it comes to being able to promote your studio with street signage. Go for a walk around your studio and look for all the potential opportunities where you could advertise your studio. Do you have windows or space on the building for you to have a sign? Maybe you have windows that are easily accessible that you could change once a month with a new promotion? If you're currently looking to move to a new venue, make sure you look out for street signage opportunities. This exposure can really help boost your leads coming through the front door. Again, have your offer on your street signage to encourage people to take action – visit your website or call you directly.

Coffee or Juice Cards

You may have noticed that some of your local cafes have loyalty cards for their regular coffee lovers. An example is that they get nine coffees and their tenth is free. I've worked with a number of dance studios on a simple campaign where you sponsor their coffee cards. Basically, the studio pays for the cards to be designed and produced, and you get one side of the card to advertise your business along with an offer. The coffee shops love this as it takes away the cost from them, plus adds more value to their clients. Your offer could lead them to your website or maybe you have them call you directly. Do a survey with your parents and ask where the best coffee in town is – and then target that coffee place!

Business Card Offer

Most studios owners I know don't have a business card. While technology is taking over slightly in this space, a business card is still an excellent way to promote your studio when you're out and about speaking with people. The biggest mistake studio owners make when getting their business cards created is that they don't place an offer on it – but an offer with a strong call to action is what drives new leads. The great thing about this is when someone says, 'Oh, my friend is looking for dance class for her child,' you can either say, 'Great! I'd be happy to give her a call and take her details,' or if you're not comfortable with that, simply give them a few cards to pass on with the offer. Now, if you want to take this to the next level, you can include an expiry date space on your business card to put the month that the offer expires – this increases the urgency to get in contact with you. I'd also give your teachers and staff business cards with the same offer that they can hand out. Just print a generic card where there is a space for them to write their name and an expiry date. Some studio owners I work with privately incentivize their staff by offering them a $50 gift voucher for anyone that comes in and enrolls in classes. It works a treat!

Lead Boxes

Lead boxes are an inexpensive yet effective way to generate new student leads. Many gyms and health clubs have been using lead boxes for years and they work. A lead box is simply a cardboard or Perspex box that has an offer on it with entry forms that you place in a complementary business to your studio within your local area – places that your students and dance families go before or after your studio, such as doctors surgeries, dance stores, coffee shops.

Firstly, you need to come up with an offer. A month of dance classes for free is a great one! Then once you've identified the perfect places to have your lead boxes, go and speak with the business owners to see if they mind you placing your box at their business. In return, you may offer them some free classes. Make sure you go and visit the lead box once a week to start with to clear out the entries, then you can see how many you get. From here you can give out one month free of classes per month and with the rest of the leads you can call them and explain that they didn't win the major prize, but you'd love to offer them two weeks of classes. Book them in and then when they come in, treat them as a new student prospect with the objective to enroll them into your classes. I love lead boxes and I've seen them work extremely well for dance studio owners.

Gift Cards

This is something you can hand out to people you meet or maybe at community performances. Really, you can hand them out anywhere. It's like a gift card you would receive from a department store, but the great thing about this is that people won't throw it in the bin. I also suggest including an expiry on these. Another great way to generate leads, these can also be handed out to your staff to circulate. These are more expensive than the business cards to produce, but a great alternative and one I recommend testing for your studio.

Bigger Budgets

Additional larger budget ways of advertising include local radio, taxis, bus shelters and television. To be honest, I've never seen a great return on these with a dance studio due to the local nature of the business. Focus your efforts on what we discussed over the last two chapters when it comes to your marketing and you'll be set!

THE NEW WAY TO WORK WITH YOUR LOCAL SCHOOLS

The way you work with and build effective relationships with schools to get them waving the flag for your studio and generate new student leads into your business has changed. You can no longer just reach out to them and ask them to hand out flyers, so I wanted to share with you how you can make this work.

First, you need to identify which schools your current students are coming from. First tip here is to include what school they go to in your online or offline enrollment form.

Next, make a list of the top 10 schools your students are coming from. Depending on what country you're from, you want to identify the schools across the different age groups where the majority of the students are from. When you create the list, you want to know the principal and deputy principals details as well as a sports coordinator. Get the contact details from one of your students or parents that attend that school if you're not sure.

Then, you'll want to approach the school. Let's talk about what you can offer the school. A big mistake that studio owners make when they're going to schools is to barge straight in with, 'Hi, how can I promote my studio to your students? Can I do an advert in your newsletter?' This is not going to build a long-term relationship with the school – this is a churn-and-burn approach which we certainly don't want. We want to think long-term relationship. So think about what you can offer the school in terms of value… a few ideas include:

Could you go and speak to students about a career in the performing arts? What it's like to work full-time as a performer and the 10 tips you can give them to prepare for working in the industry? You could do an hour-long presentation with a Q&A for the last 15 minutes. Then you could hand out free class passes or gift vouchers at the end of your presentation. This is a great way to get in. Also, you can do this for multiple age groups.

It's also a great idea to see which teachers currently teach dance for sport. There could be an opportunity here for you to supply them a teacher from your studio to teach dance for school sport. Some studios have internal dance teachers while some others have external suppliers. If they have external suppliers, ensure you keep in touch and tell them that you're interested to apply for the position when the new year starts. Teaching at the school gives you the opportunity to really build a solid relationship with the students and teachers. You can encourage the school to feature the students at the assembly where the rest of the students would see them, as well as perform representing the school in the community. This then promotes the school as well as your studio. It's a win-win situation. They could run school concerts or musicals that you or your teachers could help with. This is also another great opportunity to get in with the school and build a relationship.

I'm not saying you do any of this for free, besides the career talk. The rest would be paid work, but more than that it's about building the relationships with the schools. Many studio owners tell me that they've tried to build relationships with the schools but rarely have they spoken to the right people and offered the value up front. The other thing is that you need to be persistent with the schools as they have other priorities, so you need to ensure you're helping them out first.

Once you make the initial approach with the school principal, deputy and/or sports coordinator, keep in touch with them every 90 days. Maybe it's around a birthday or you've seen that the school has performed really well at a sports competition or in an academic way. This will ensure you and your studio stay top of mind all the time.

Once you have built the relationship and have given value to the school, then you can speak with them about advertising your studio in their newsletter. This is only part of the strategy and over the years I've seen this work extremely well with the studios that have a long-standing relationship with the school.

This process has been proven time and time again with studio owners and it's a great way to engage with your local schools to have them become a great referral machine for your studio. Sure, it takes a little bit of work, but in the long run this will certainly pay off!

GET PEOPLE INSIDE YOUR STUDIO – OPEN HOUSE/DAY

It's one thing for people to have a look on your website, but it's another to get your prospective students and their families in the door. Running an open day once a quarter and more in the lead up to the new dance year is a fantastic way to promote your studio to the local community. From running free workshops to uniform fashion parades and talks from experts, in this chapter I'll share with you the steps for creating an open day that generates new leads and boosts your studio culture.

Many studios organise open days or houses when they start off the new dance year but many don't leverage the opportunity as much as they could or should. You see, by running these events you can get a large amount of people through your doors that generally wouldn't have the opportunity to see what you do! Not to mention it's great to run these events to re-enroll current students into the new year.

Let's run through the different types of open day or open house events you can put on at your studio.

2-hour Mini Open House/Day

You may want to run this each week on a different afternoon, the month leading up to the new dance year starting. These mini events simply give potential new students and their parents the opportunity to come and see your studio, as well as meet you and your teachers and ask any questions they have about enrolling for classes. You should always get a number of teachers to come along to these events. Your teachers are the backbone of the studio, so it's very important that they are there speaking with the people who are interested in your classes. By having the teachers there, it also shows parents and students the level of commitment your teachers have. During this event I would encourage you to set up one or two televisions that can play vision of your classes, competitions or recitals. You may even want to cut together a five-minute reel that showcases all of the different aspects of your studio: your classes, teachers, highlights of your achievements over the years. You can just put this on a loop so it continues playing. This doesn't need to cost you the world, either – jump onto Elance or Fiverr and get a great looking reel at an affordable price. Just make sure you spend time creating a detailed brief that they can follow. You also want them to use royalty free music so you can use it everywhere you like.

During the two-hour event, you will need to make sure that you have everything on hand that a new enrollment needs to make their decision. You'll need enrollment forms (some studios are doing only enrollments through their management software which can be done via an ipad or tablet, which is very convenient.) You'll also need on hand any information like timetables, rules and regulations, uniform price lists to give them when they sign up. Also make sure you have enrollment gifts ready to hand out on the day. I also encourage you to ask if they'd like to organize their uniform then. Some studios I work with say to the new family that if they purchase their uniform today then they will halve the enrollment or registration fee. Not everyone will register as a student on the day, so the most important thing is to make sure you get contact details so that you can add them to your newsletter. Think about when you go to view a house to rent or buy, and the real estate agent will ask for your contact details – it's the same thing here. They will then receive your newsletter making sure your studio stays top of mind! You may also like to have some balloons out the front of the studios and inside the studio to create a more energetic environment. These should be very low cost events to you, but highly effective in confirming new student enrollments.

Super Sized Open Day/House

Your other option is to run a 4-6 hour open day or open house where you have special things happening across the day. This is a much larger event that you can run two or four times per year. It's as much about new student acquisition as it is retention of current students, and generally works best on a Saturday between 10-2 or 10-4pm. As with the small event, ensure you have all new enrollment materials available, but also run a number of other things during the day. Create a schedule that you can email out as well as share on social media. As this is a big event, you should spend some time working out your strategy for marketing it. Start marketing four weeks out from the event by emailing your current student list encouraging them to share the event with their friends. Not only can they forward on the email, they can also promote the event through social media. Give them access to a Facebook cover photo that you'll have designed that they can upload to their profile. Current students love to get involved in these events, so give them all the promotional materials they need to promote the event. You could even run a promotion where you say bring along one friend to the open day or open house event to receive one weeks' worth of classes free. The parents love that one! This would run separately to your referral program, which we will talk about in an upcoming module. Other ways to promote the event is through paid Facebook adverts, strategic partners through distributing flyers and posters and a direct mail campaign. If you're putting the time and energy into running this event ensure you spend the time really getting it out there. Be proactive and really look at every promotional opportunity that is going to provide you with an excellent outcome.

The other thing is that you don't need to organise this all on your own. Get your office staff and teachers involved in making this happen. They will love being a part of this!

More Ways To Create An Awesome Open Day/House
Here are some ideas for great things you can do on the day:

Face painting – Speak with a local birthday party business and ask them to supply one or two people who can come, dress up and paint faces for a few hours. In return they can promote their parties on the day and will be included in the promotional material.

Workshops – You can run a few workshops with your current awesome teachers, or maybe you want to look at getting a guest teacher or two in that has a profile and will bring more students through the door. If you bring in a guest teacher, make sure that as part of the deal, they promote that they will be appearing at the open event and include the poster with the details. In regards to the classes you offer, offer the ones that are most popular across a number of age groups. For example, it could be a jazz class for ages 6-10, 10-13 and 14+. Make sure you get loads of photos of the workshops that you and your students can share on social media. Allow 10 minutes after the workshop for photos.

Class viewings – If you're running your open day on a Saturday, during a regular dance week have a number of classes that are open, which means people who are interested in coming to see one of your dance classes in action are able to. Make sure you get written permission from the parents previously. It's best to include this on your enrollment form so you don't need to get additional paperwork filled out.

Q&A teacher panel – In between a workshop or class, you may want to hold a 20- minute Q&A panel with you and a few teachers. Here people can ask you questions about the studio, but also about having a career in the industry. This is great for your current students and potential new students and their families.

Expert talk (future career in the entertainment industry) – You may also like the person who takes your workshop to do a 20-30 minute Q&A where students and parents can ask them questions about their experience and career. There's a lot of value in this and people love hearing inspiring stories from people they admire and want to be like. If it's okay with the person, you could video parts of the talk and post them on your website and social media accounts.

Uniform fashion parade – Some studios offer modelling, so this is a great one for them. Have a fashion parade that shows off your uniform. Even if you don't offer modelling, this can be a great addition to your event as it gives your students something really fun to be part of while promoting your uniform range. You may also like to do a special for the day where if they spend, for example $100, they'll receive something for free like a top or dance bag.

Prizes from local businesses – It's always fun if you can give out prizes during the day and what better place to look for prizes than from local businesses. Go to your local beautician, hairdresser, car wash, gym or similar and see if they will donate a prize for the day. In return, you can provide them with advertising on the day and on the promotional material.

Now it's your turn to start planning your next open day or open house. I encourage you to open your diary and lock in some dates that will work so you can start getting them underway. Remember, you ideally want to run one small event a week for four weeks and a larger event 2-4 times per year.

STAND OUT FROM THE PACK - POSITIONING AND PUBLICITY

Local publicity is still very much alive and media outlets are always on the lookout for great content – it's just that the old school way of newspaper editorials aren't the most effective avenue to travel down.

What Is Publicity?

Some people get publicity confused with advertising, but they are completely the opposite. When you think of advertising, I'm sure TV ads, radio ads, print ads, banner adverts and billboards come to mind. Advertising is a way to market your studio that you pay for and generally at a premium price, yet publicity is absolutely free and allows your message to get out there in front of your target market.

The cool thing about publicity is that it's way more effective than advertising. Sounds strange, right... the thing that is free is more effective than the thing that costs you money. There are many benefits to publicity that I'd love to share with you now:

Greater credibility – We all know an advertisement when we see one. We know the company has paid for it and know that whatever the ad says has been created by the company that owns the service or product. So, as a consumer, we can become a little bit sceptical. The great thing about publicity is that it's believable as it's coming from another source and we think that if a news source is talking about it, then the company must be doing something worthwhile.

Publicity reaches a wider audience. The great thing is that if you get coverage in one publication, the story could get picked up by another, meaning that more people will read about you and your studio.

It's cost effective – I said before that it's free, but if you take into account the phone calls you need to make to speak with journalists or bloggers and include the time you spend doing that, it's not entirely free – but it is much less than placing an advert somewhere for your studio.

It has longevity – An advert lasts as long as you continue paying for it, but publicity can stay around much longer. Thanks to the internet and monthly publications, your story will last and will be remembered far longer than an advert.

How To Cut Through

So, the big question from our Studio Success Formula program members, when we first start discussing publicity, is how can they get publicity when there are loads of other dance studios in their area? It's competitive and every studio is vying for the attention and for the local media to run their stories. They feel like they don't have any unique angles to offer the media. This is certainly not true. Whether you're a studio that's been around for 20 years or just started this year, you will have a number of stories that your local media would pick up. The media has one main objective when it comes to content and that's about keeping their audience engaged and continually consuming their resource whether it's a blog, website, newspaper, magazine, radio station, podcast or similar.

How To Get Media Exposure

Let's now run through the steps of how you can secure media exposure for your studio. Here are the 7 steps to generating free publicity for your business:

1. Define what makes your studio unique - What's the difference between your studio versus the other studios in your local area? Create just a few lines or bullet points that clearly explain why you do what you do.

2. Declare your outcomes – Many studio owners say they want publicity, but when I ask them what results they are after from the publicity, they're not really sure. As with all of your marketing efforts, you always need to have well-defined goals when executing a piece of marketing... how many new student leads you want, how many do you want to convert to students etc. It's the same with publicity. List 3-5 objectives you want to achieve by rolling out your publicity campaigns. It could be 50 new student enquiries, increase enquiries through the website by 10%, create a higher profile for the studio within the local community. Sit down and brainstorm these with your staff so that you all get on the same page.

3. Revisit your ideal student avatars – Who do you want to target when creating your publicity campaign? Get really clear on who you want to be engaged in your campaign roll-outs and link it back to your core objectives.

4. Create your media target list – Now that you know what your objectives are and who you want to target, you need to do some research to identify who the right media contacts are to approach and get your story out there! Some studios do a scatter gun approach, sending it to everyone which is not a great idea. The media love it when something relevant lands on their desk or in their inbox. What they don't like is getting a media release that has nothing to do with what they write about. It's beyond important that you do your research thoroughly to

ensure your news gets into the hands of the right person who can do something useful with it. Even if you have to call the media outlet to find out who the best person is to send the media release to, then do it! LinkedIn is also a great place to search for the right people to speak with within your local community media. Now for this you want to identify 10-15 people within media companies that you could pitch your stories to. As I mentioned before, look at blogs, newspapers, magazines, news websites, local radio stations, local television stations. The list is really endless, but you just need to find the select few who will be really excited to hear from you because it's exactly what they're after!

5. Build your story angles – Now comes the fun part. Get together with your team, partner or mentor and start brainstorming your story angles. This is a two-fold approach: the first one is to discuss what you currently have happening in the studio and the second is what you'd like to do that could get you placement in the media. As an example, maybe you have a graduate student that is in a musical at the moment. You could certainly pitch a story to your local media about this and they would be interested. You'd need to speak with the show's publicist first. Another angle might be that you run a special class once a month that is targeted at children under 15 who have a disability. You then want to think about the next 6-12 months and what you'd like to roll out that will generate you some publicity. Maybe you'll donate a percentage of your concert or recital profits to a local charity or you'll have a celebrity dance guest to do a workshop with your students. You could even talk about heading to a new city or country to compete in a big competition. The aim here is to come up with 10 ideas knowing that they won't all get picked up giving you a good mix to work with.

6. Write your media release – no longer than one page. Then pitch your idea – it's now time to send your media release out to the suitable media contacts on your pitch list. Include your media release in the body of the email as well as a word document attachment. Make sure you also include any high resolution images that support your media release.

7. Follow up – Four days after you have sent the release, follow up with a phone call to see if they require any further information. If they don't

answer leave them a voicemail message and follow up with an email saying that you called. Then leave it a week until you contact them again. It's important you get them on the phone to check in to see if they are running the story or not.

Now, some of the studios I've worked with over the years have decided to bring on board a publicity consultant to help them in coming up with ideas and then pitching these ideas to the media. You can certainly engage a consultant to help you, but it's important that you get the right type of person who understands local media, has existing contacts and knows something about the dance industry.

BECOMING COMMUNITY FOCUSED

Reaching out to your local community, showcasing your studio and assisting local charities where suitable, all form part of your yearly community strategy. From performing at local events to raising money for local charities, there are multiple ways to give back to the community while raising awareness of your studio and generating new business and student enquiries.

So let me ask you right now – how much time a week do you spend on community-focused activities? I understand that you're probably time poor, but it's super important that you're dedicating a small amount of time each week to nurture your community relationships and really maximize every opportunity you have to raise the awareness of your studio and classes and get people enquiring about them.

The Magic Word Is LEVERAGE

Many studio owners come to us having already tried community outreach with very little return on their time and money investment. The truth here is that they didn't leverage each opportunity; today I'm going to explain to you exactly what leverage means and how you can do it effectively to really increase your results.

So why do community marketing in the first place? That's an excellent question and probably one you're asking if you have tried a bunch of localised marketing strategies, but they've never felt like they're worthwhile due to their time commitment and, sometimes, money investment.

Let's discuss the benefits of getting out into your community and showcasing your school:

Super targeted – The majority of people you'll be speaking with are local to your area, meaning there's a higher chance of them coming along to a class than doing a broad marketing piece.

Increase referrals and recommendations – Your current students are able to tell their friends about what you're up to. If you're performing at a local fair they can promote this to their networks and get them down to watch.

Retention – If you're performing at a local event, this is a great opportunity for your students to do what they love – performing. The parents will love this and will not only be grateful to you for the opportunity, but it will make them more loyal to your studio. It's about creating a tribe, and by bringing your students together outside of their regular class environment, you will certainly accelerate this process.

Brand awareness – The more you get out and do things in the community, the more people will start to recognize your studio name. Make sure you have a striking uniform that students wear to all performances and class. This will increase the interest in your studio, which in turn will boost the amount of enquiries coming into your business.

Giving back – It feels great to give back to your local community – and it's even better if you can include your students in the process. You may go to a nursing home to perform a few Christmas songs in December and spend some time with sick people in a home.

Let's get into the types of things you can do within your community to give back while generating new business! You'll see here that I'm going to talk about what you can do and then I'm going to explain how you can take the opportunity to the next level by using the concept of leverage.

For me, leverage means taking an existing opportunity and slicing it up to really maximize the opportunity. Remember to always review your ideal student avatars when approaching these strategies. You want to make sure there's always a match. Meaning that your ideal students and parents are going to see or be a part of the community activity you get involved with.

Sponsor local activities such as kids or adult sports teams, school events, church activities, hospitals, meet ups and networking events. You may give away a term or month of dancing or a ten-class pass, as an example. Now to leverage this opportunity, ensure you get a link to your studio on their website. It would also be great to include your logo and a short blurb about your studio on their site. If you're sponsoring an event, ask if you can have promotional material at the event, maybe even a table where you can talk to people about your studio. I'd also ask to be included in any emails that get sent out pre and post the event which includes a link back to your website. You could also do a special offer for the people on their list which provides them with more value for their customers.

Perform at local events, whether it be a fair or an opening of a shopping mall. Maximize the opportunity by handing out flyers or cards for your studio with a strong call to action and expiry date. As an example, you might offer seven days of classes for free, but it has to be used within the month. Encourage these people to take action quickly, this will greatly increase your conversion rate.

Engage your dance families in volunteer activities around four times per year. For a few hours, round up a group of students and parents to go and feed the hungry or maybe work in a community garden or animal shelter. Get loads of photos while you're there to share on your website and social media and see if the local media would cover the story.

Choreograph for local groups to get in front of more of your ideal students. It might be for the community musical theatre group or similar. Either you or one of your dedicated teachers would be great to get involved. It's a fantastic way to give back, promote your work and increase new student enquiries.

Offer local schools a special offer for any students that sign up for classes with you. This would be exclusive for the schools. Maybe they would receive some free merchandise on sign-up or similar. If possible, ask the school to promote this offer through their newsletter, social media and website with links back to your studio.

Give support for local charity organizations and ask them to put your link on their website as a supporter. In addition to the links this strategy builds trust for your business. You want this to be a long-term strategy. Work on a year-long strategy with them that includes you providing them with dancers for special events or similar.

Right there, you have six community strategies you can start putting into place immediately. Now, don't try and do all of them. I suggest if you can do one thing a month, that would be awesome – you would certainly see an increase in enquiries, plus you'll increase current student loyalty and the overall happiness of your studio by giving back.

STRATEGIC PARTNERSHIPS

We can't talk about offline marketing and community involvement without going into strategic partnerships. A strategic partnership is a formal agreement between two or more complementary businesses, often formed to build stronger and desirable market positions for the parties involved.

So basically, it means you form a relationship with a business that also serves your ideal students and/or parents, but they are not a competitor and you work on a plan together to increase brand awareness and new business enquiries. There is generally no money exchanged and the relationship needs to be mutually beneficial so that everyone wins.

What benefits do we get from putting in place strategic relationships with local businesses? Let me tell you right now the top four reasons you want to work on building strategic partners today!

1. Access to complementary services. Let's say you form a relationship with a local singing school. As you only offer dance, you can refer people both ways which is perfect, as dance and singing goes hand-in-hand. You're not interested in offering singing lessons, but you will be able to offer a solution to students who want to sing as well as dance – meaning you won't lose that student to an all singing and dancing studio.

2. Opportunity to reach new markets. Maybe only a small percentage of your student base comes from a particular city; you can form a relationship with a local business who serves moms in that area. This means your studio is reaching people who generally wouldn't have known you existed.

3. Increase Brand Awareness. While increasing awareness doesn't always result in someone taking action immediately, if they see your studio enough continually, they will start to take more notice, which increases your chances of them reaching out to you.

4. Boost in Sales & Audience – This is the greatest benefit of creating a strategic partnership. It's going to boost your new student enrollments and build your audience. The great thing about this is you only need to have a handful of strong strategic relationships to bring handfuls of enquiries into your studio each week.

It's important to point out here that there are a few challenges with securing the right type of strategic partnership that you need to be aware of:

No trust – Your gut is not just there to digest your food – it's also there to guide you with decision making. You know when you meet someone and you either warm to them quickly, or you think to yourself that there's something off about them? This applies to finding the right people to form a strategic partnership with. You need to trust one another. Think of it as a marriage; without trust you have nothing. Without trust, you won't refer them new business, nor will they refer students to you. Make sure there is loads of trust there and that you remain transparent.

No drive – Both parties need to be passionate about making the relationship work. You both need to be drivers. It doesn't work if one partner is driving all the activity while the other one sits back and relaxes.

Lack of resources – As a small business, I know you don't have loads of resources to be promoting other peoples' business and I'll address that very soon. You know what resources you do have though, so when you negotiate what's involved in the partnership, be honest and transparent. Know what you can handle and what you can't and be open about this. Your partner will appreciate it!

Different values – Again, I relate this to a romantic relationship. The relationships where partners have conflicting values don't last, and this is the same with strategic partnerships. Make sure you're on the same page in regards to your values.

5 STEPS TO CREATE STRATEGIC PARTNERSHIPS

So now you know the benefits and the challenges to beware of, let me walk you through the five steps of how to set up your strategic partnership.

1. Have a clear vision for your business. Where do you see your business headed? What do you want for your studio? It's important that you're clear, as a switched-on partner will want to know this. This also sets up the foundation for the partnership.

2. What are your immediate business goals? What do you want for your business over the next 90 days? Maybe it's new student enquiries. Come up with 1-3 goals you want to achieve over the next 90 days.

3. Determine how a strategic partner could help – What could they do for you so that you can reach your goals. We'll talk about some examples shortly, but you can get really creative here.

Determine your strengths and capabilities – What can you offer a partner? Maybe you have a large student and parent database or a big following on Facebook, or you could be connected to the local community. Come up with a list of strengths and capabilities that you can bring to the table.

4. Brainstorm and create a list of potential partners. Let your imagine run wild here. Think about your current students and parents. Where are they going before and after they come to class? These are the businesses you want to approach as there will be people just like them there! Get together with your team, your partner or speak with parents and get a list of about 20 businesses to start with and number them in order of the ones you really want up the top.

5. The approach – Once you've done this, it's time to approach the business owners and start to build a relationship with them. If you already have a relationship with them, that's great, but if you don't, then you need to start. This is a crucial part of the process. You simply can't rock up to a business owner and say, 'Hi, do you want to promote each others' business?'

I'm a big believer in giving value. By giving value upfront, people are more likely to engage with you on a deeper level. The approach I created, which has worked with my private mentoring clients, is around you creating a VIP directory of local businesses that you promote to your studio families. This directory can be on paper as well as online and lists a number of local businesses that you support. These businesses can include gyms, hair dressers, beauty salons, cafes, real estate agents, florists, pre-schools, singing studios, doctors carwashes, nutritionists, lawyers, Pilates or yoga studios and the list goes on. Basically, anything you know your families would find valuable. You would approach your ideal business list introducing yourself and mentioning that you have a range of parents and/or students that use their services and you'd love to include them on your local business directory that you're promoting at your studio. No one will say no to this. You may also like to ask them if they'd like to promote a special offer for their business to encourage your families to test them out. Again, most business owners will give you a special offer for your families.

At this point you gather the details you need and tell them that you'll be in touch. What I love about this approach is that it's all about them and you're wanting to provide more value to your students and their families. Now, you can do this via a phone call or email, but as they are local, I prefer a face-to-face hello. If they are busy, you can simply email them and follow up with a phone call. Aim to have the directory up and happening within two weeks. You should be able to turn this around quite quickly. I would then give them a call when the directory has launched and then two weeks later give them another call to check in. This is where you make an offer to them where you can give them a bunch of gift cards for their clients that gives them two weeks free of classes or similar. You can come up with the offer, and they will jump at the offer as it's a way they can give additional value to their customers plus you've already done something for them so they'll naturally want to do something for you. This is called the rule of reciprocity. From here you would organize the offer and to get some business cards or gift cards made up that they can offer to their clients. Over the years, working with studios I've found this to be the most effective way to start a strategic partnership relationship. From there you can do a number of cool things with your partners to generate more enquiries as well as local press.

Here are a few ideas that have worked with my private studio owner clients in regards to activities they've done with their strategic partners:

Real Estate Agents

Generally, a real estate agent gives a pack to new homeowners or new renters that has information in it about the local area. You could include a postcard in this pack that offers their new family the opportunity to come to classes. I've done a Brady Bunch type of card with photos of our parents and students that says... *New In Town? Join our dance family.* It's worked extremely well and, again, has an expiry on the offer for the month that they move in.

Gyms or Personal Trainers

Many gyms have open days where they invite all their members down to do classes with guest instructors or team competitions. A great idea is to have a table at these events where you can promote your studio and classes. You may even offer to teach a special dance class for their members. It could even be a Mummy and Me class where members bring along their toddlers. This is a great opportunity for you then to get them to come along to a preschool class at your studio.

Carwash

Depending on where your studio is based, I've worked with studios who work with their partner car wash to create an offer that hangs from the rear-vision mirror in the car so when they pick up their car there is an offer there for them to redeem that is transferable so they can give it away.

Team Class

You may want to offer your strategic partners the opportunity to come for a jazz class altogether, so they can meet each other, exercise and network. These work really well and further cement your relationship with everyone. Alternatively, you may just want to organize a networking event at your studio and invite a few speakers to come along and present on strategies for small business owners.

Pre-School Classes

Speak with your pre-school partner and offer to go in there and help choreograph a dance for a show where their parents come to watch.

Singing Studio

For your concert or recital you might like to invite the local singing studio along to perform a few numbers. This will be great for both businesses as their students and parents will see what you're all about and vice versa.

I can't encourage you enough to start the wheels in motion to get a handful of strategic partners up and running. The main point here is that it's all about building relationships. If you invest a small amount of time in this strategy you will see a huge return on your investment. The other great thing about strategic partnerships is that they don't cost you money!

Chapter Ten

CREATE RAVING FANS WHO REFER

'Loyal customers, they don't just come back,
they don't simply recommend you, they insist that their friends
do business with you.' ~ Chip Bell

When I first start working with our program members, I always ask where their enrollments are coming from, and 90% of the time they will say word of mouth. Your students and parents talking to their friends and family members about your studio is the best type of publicity you could get! So here's the problem… it's where we're getting the most amount of our new students from, but it's where we spend the least amount of time. Well, today we are going to change that as I hand you over my formula for creating a rock solid and highly popular referral program.

Firstly, I want you to think about how many referrals you've received over the last 12 months in your studio from existing parents and students. If you don't know this number, I encourage you to find it out straight away, along with your top five referring families. You know I love the numbers, so I want you to know these figures as they are important. You see, let's say Mrs Jones has referred you six new students who have stayed for a year. This could be worth over $5,000 to you depending on how many classes they do and your pricing structure.

Imagine if you could just bump up your referrals by 10-20% over the next six months... how much of an impact this could make on your business including your bank balance?

Right now, with those top five referrals in mind, I want you to start identifying why you believe they are sending students to you. What makes them a raving fan for your business and what is it that you're doing in your studio that makes them want to tell everyone about you? This exercise in itself is extremely powerful.

I can tell you now that the answer isn't simply because you provide great dance classes. Perhaps these are parents and students who spend quite a bit of time at the studio, so they've gotten to know you as a business owner, but more importantly as a real person. I'm going to share with you some effective strategies for boosting word of mouth in an upcoming lesson which is really exciting, but for now It's time to talk about your referral program.

DO YOU HAVE A REFERRAL PROGRAM?

I'd love for you to put your hand up right now if you have a referral program in place at the moment. Now look, I know many of you are going to have your hand up halfway because you do but you don't. Let me explain – you kinda have this thing in place where if one of your existing parents or students refers a new student who stays for two months or a term, then you reward them with something, but you've never promoted it and you have a system in place that consistently rewards those people that do refer.

I get it my friends, and that's totally okay because I'm giving you a system so you can implement a referral program into your studio. I'm just going to share with you the most effective system I've used with studio owners, as I know it works and more importantly it works quickly!

Now let's jump into my referral card formula.

THE REFERRAL CARD

I love the referral card. Many gyms, health clubs, day cares, financial services and other service based business use them. It's a business card sized card (make sure it's no bigger) that you can hand out to parents and students for them to hand to prospective students. I mentioned cards earlier and giving them to your teachers to refer is the same initial concept, only for your dance families who are taking classes.

Sounds simple so far, hey? But you need to be careful with the next step as this will determine the programs that will work and the ones that won't. You need to have the card professionally designed by a graphic designer. I have seen studio owners print cards that have been created in Microsoft Word, are black and white and have been printed on regular paper. I'm sorry, but this is a massive no no – not only will the cards get wrecked in the wallets and purses of your parents, they won't want to be handing out some cheap looking card, will they? This is why I strongly encourage you to spend the small amount of money to get a great looking card that promotes your studio's brand in the best light possible.

What's On The Referral Card?

Let's talk about what you need to place on the card. On the front of the card, you need an electrifying design that has your studio logo, an image plus the words, 'You're invited.' That's it!

Now from all the work we've done together over these last 10 chapters, what are your thoughts about what the image should be? The one thing I focus on when a studio is executing its marketing plan is to ensure their campaign is relevant to the target market they are after, so yes, you guessed it – you're going to have multiple cards done with an image that is relevant for the person who receives the card.

Segmenting Is Crucial

You're printing this at the normal business card size, so the cost is going to be extremely low as you'll be using the same layout with your designer for the cards so they will just need to switch in the new images. Now for the different age groups, you want to target dance styles. I like to do the following age groups 2-5 years old, 6-10 years old, 11-13 years old and then 14+. I then want you to select the most popular dance style for that age group and use that as a guide for each image. It's best if you use images from your studio as it's much more personal than a stock image, but if you don't have any of your students and don't have a photographer or a parent who could take some happy snaps for you, then simply head to dollarphotoclub.com and you can download photos from there to use for only $1 each. It's pretty cool!

You're Invited

In regards to the copy saying 'You're Invited'... this is because the person who is giving them a card is essentially inviting them to classes with you. We love receiving something in the mail and an email with the words you're invited; it makes us feel special and that it's only for us. I've tested multiple versions of this card with different copy, and I'm giving you the absolute killer version right here that has had the highest new student conversion rate.

Next, we want to flip over the card and get onto what we'll actually have on the back of the card!

So here we go... The back of the card should read:

Date: top right hand side.

Hi (Name of Referred Student) (you leave a space for them to write it in)

I'd love to offer you the opportunity to come along and experience (Dance Studio Name) by giving you this 7-day unlimited class pass. That's right, you can come along and do any classes you like for 7 days as a gift from me. Simply email (Email Address) or call (Phone Number) within the month to book in for the classes you'd love to attend.

Hope to see you in class soon!

(Students Full Name)

Studio Website Address

Easy as that! The back of the card should be white with black text so that it's easy to read. It's a personal message and it's not all sales like, but includes all the important bits, like the make contact within this month part, so they take action quickly and the fact that it's a gift, not a freebie.

There's nothing else to having the card designed. If you follow this format, you'll be well on your way to generating a truckload of additional referrals. Check out moo.com and vistaprint.com to get your cards printed cheaply.

HOW TO INCENTIVIZE YOUR DANCE FAMILIES

I now want to discuss with you the options for how you can incentivize your dance families for spreading the word about your studio through this program. I'm going to give you a few ideas for what you can offer and some things will sit better with you than others. I want you to select the one that works for you and your dance families best and go with that!

- $25 off your term/two months fees when you refer a friend who signs up and pays for a term/two months. You can do this with any amount. I have studios that go up to $50 because the acquisition of a new student is worth that for them. Firstly, work out what your average student pays you a year and then work out the amount you're happy to discount your existing student for a referral.

- Similar to the above, you can pass on the discount to both the referrer and the referee. So you might take off $25 off fees for your current student and then $25 off term fees or fees when they pay two months upfront to the new student. This has worked extremely well with many of our studios, as it's a nice surprise after they have done their one week's worth of classes and are ready to join. It can also help with those who are on the fence about enrolling. The important thing here is that you get at least a term or two months of fees paid and then provide the discount.

- $25 off your costume fee for the concert or recital when you refer a friend. Parents really appreciate this one as every little bit helps when it comes to paying for costumes.

- Spin the referral wheel – when you refer a friend who signs up and pays for term/two months. Let me explain because I'm in love with the Referral Wheel. Basically, it's a wheel – like wheel of fortune, but better! You have a wheel made; one of your studio dads could do this and you have prizes on the wheel that they can win from referring new students. Some ideas I love for the wheel include money off fees, private lesson, merchandise, gift voucher for a café or dance store. The options really are limitless and this isn't the most important part. The kids love spinning the wheel and so do the parents, and it also shows your other dance families that you have a referral program. You can't go past the wheel in my eyes. You can also have the new students spin the wheel if you'd like to pass that gift on to them.

- Provide them with a bonus gift for every fifth person they refer. My favorite incentive is a $100 credit towards their fees. This one is up to you, but it's great when they refer three people, then they can see that five is so close so they push to get there. It's super cool and effective.

- Also, each year you may like to run a competition where everyone who refers five or more people receives a ticket into the draw to win a year's worth of tuition. There is no limit to the amount of people they can refer, so every five people that they refer will receive a ticket into the draw, increasing their chances.

SOME TERMS AND CONDITIONS

Okay now, let's not forget the terms and conditions. As with every referral program, we need to ensure that there are some rules in place so that everyone is on the same page.

- There is no limit to the amount of new students you refer

- The offer applies to new students only or students who have not danced at the studio for at least 12 months

- A referral card must be filled out (please go to the office to grab one). Referring students will be determined by the name written in the "referred by" portion of the referral card.

- You will also need to include how the incentive works. As an example you would write 'Once your referral enrolls and pays for a term or two months worth of classes, then your account will be credited $50.'

One last piece of advice – tracking is really important when implementing a solid referral program. Depending on what software system you use, you need to ensure that you're keeping track of who is referring whom. It's a simple task but one that often gets missed – so stay on top of it.

PROMOTING YOUR REFERRAL PROGRAM

Once you have your referral program created, it's time to get your promotional plan in place so people actually know about it to really drive your word of mouth strategy further than it's ever gone before.

Before we dive into the referral promotion pool, there are a few things you need to know when it comes to referrals. Your parents and students will only start raving about your studio once you've developed trust, built a relationship, done something different, gone above and beyond expectations for the parent and/or student or provided an exceptional service. So, sure, it can take some time to generate results through a referral program with new students, but you can certainly be getting some big wins with the dance families who have been with you for a while and know exactly how you operate.

As I've mentioned repeatedly, having a referral program is one of the best marketing strategies and opportunities for studio owners looking to take their business to the next level. I've seen word of mouth marketing and having a solid referral policy in place completely transform the businesses of many studio owners who have gone through the program.

Okay, so let's start discussing how you can get the word out there about your referral program

1. ASK – Sounds like a no-brainer, right? Well, it is, but it's the biggest thing that people miss and as a studio owner, you're presented with opportunities every day to ask them for referrals. As an example, Mrs Jones comes up to you and says, 'Mr Clint, I just wanted to say how much Julie is loving classes. She's made some really lovely friends and I catch her practicing in her bedroom. Her face lights up on dancing days, so thank you for all that you do.' Who doesn't love this kind of feedback? What you could say back to that is, 'Wow, Mrs Smith, that's awesome to hear and that's the exact reason I started the studio in the first place. Julie is a pleasure to teach, great energy and filled with joy, and I'm so glad she's been able to make some new friends. Mrs Smith, just thinking about what you said, have you heard about our referral

program we have here? I'd love to give you some cards to hand out when you come across one of Julie's friends who might like to come along as well. We also reward our families that refer by giving them X.' Now obviously you would need to take a breath here and ask them questions so it becomes a two-way conversation, but I'm sure you get my drift. Now, you asking doesn't need to be limited by just face-to-face encounters – you can also do this over the phone and via email. Easy as!

2. Have a poster – When your designer is creating your cards, also have them design a poster for you that promotes the referral program to your current dance families. You can then print and place these posters around the studio as well as send the poster out in emails. If you have a special membership part of your website, you can also include it here and on social media. More on all of this shortly, but the one thing to take away here is to create a poster.

3. Newsletter promotion – The regular newsletter that you send out to your dance families is the best way to promote your referral program. You can certainly put the poster in the newsletter, but there are a few other ways you can talk about the program. Firstly, you can do a shout out to all the people who have referred new students and say a big thank you, and secondly you may talk about one person who has referred a large amount of new students and the money they have saved – like a mini case study. It's important that your dance families are continually reminded of the benefits of promoting your referral program. Make sure you mention how they can claim their referral cards, too.

4. Post your referral cards – For all new students, I suggest you post them a personal letter after they have been at your studio for two weeks to check in with them, tell them that you hope they are having an awesome time and if they are, then you'd love for them to share that with their friends. Enclose five of your referral cards and make sure you say that they can collect more from the office and that you appreciate their support.

5. Social Media – I encourage you to promote your referral program on your closed Facebook group and also talk about the families who

have been referring new students. For example, you may take a photo of your current student and new student that says… Thanks Emily for referring your friend Sophie to us. Love welcoming new families to our studio! #referafriend.

Your dance families can promote your studio in conversations at dinner parties or while waiting to pick up their children from school, maybe at a school event or at a family gathering.

What I wanted to finish with is how you can utilize social media to have your raving fans promote your studio online. I mean, social media platform is just word of mouth powered by technology. My favorite strategy for doing this is through running monthly promotions on Facebook. Each month, create a themed promotion with the objective to increase engagement with your current students, but also allows them to engage with their social networks.

The first thing to do is to create a studio cover photo for your students. Don't include images of students in this as you will never to be able to get everyone in a photo, so just make it a brand piece of artwork that includes your logo, website and a statement. Some examples include:

I Heart (Studio Initials)
I'm A (Studio Name) Kid

The other option you have for the statement is to make it a quote about dance and life. These have proven to be extremely popular with dance students.

Once you have created the cover photo, send an email to your studio families telling them that you've created a new cover photo and for them to feel free to upload it to their Facebook profile for the month. Also include this information in your closed Facebook group and during the month comment on the people who have it up.

Promote monthly

Now, in regards to the promotions each month, this runs in line with referrals, but it's actually a competition. For example, it's the month of Mother's Day. You could do a fun promotion playing on the US television show Dance Moms, where you would say we're looking for the best dance moms during this month for mothers' day. Simply upload a photo of you and your mum and tell us in 25 words or less why you have the best dance mum. Make sure you also include Studio Name Page at the end of your post and #bestmum. The person who receives the most likes from their friends will receive one month of classes for free. That's just an example, though – the promotion and the prize are completely up to you.

You may want to alternate the Facebook cover photo with the competition to keep it fresh and exciting. Plan these six months in advance so you're prepared and don't drop the ball.

On another note, make sure you thank your dance families when they refer someone. You might send an email telling them how to redeem their prize or credit but you may also send just a nice, handwritten card and pop it in the mail. A simple thank you goes a long way, so don't forget to do this at the end of the process.

There you have it. A number of strategies to ensure your awesome referral programs gets the exposure it deserves while really supersizing the referrals generated from your dance families.

Chapter Eleven

STUDENTS THAT STAY (YOUR RETENTION ROADMAP)

'Your customer doesn't care how much you know until they know how much you care.' ~ Damon Richards

First up, let's get through the tricky subject of effective communication. As a studio owner, we are continually communicating with our students and parents and the ways in which communication comes in and goes out varies. There's email, phone calls, text messages, Facebook private profile messages, Facebook page messages, Facebook group messages, written letters, newsletters… and it doesn't stop there. Much of the time, I'm sure you feel like you never have the chance to turn off. Nothing ever goes away, which means you always feel like you need to be connected 24/7 – but the truth is, you don't.

If you feel like this, my thoughts are that you allow this to happen. You might not have set any boundaries or expectations, which means people are always wanting a reply urgently. Does this sound familiar?

The one thing to remember is that when someone is contacting you, they are pushing their own agenda, and what I've seen over and over again with my private studio owner clients is that they're continually taking calls and emails throughout the day – meaning they're not really working productively. The constant interruptions = no high priority tasks getting done. So what's the big thing I want you to take away from this revelation? That you don't need to answer every email and phone call that very second – in fact, it's detrimental to your business if you do this.

Although this chapter is not about productivity, we are talking about effective communication – and effective communication is all about being efficient and productive!

7 CORE WAYS PEOPLE LEARN

So, first we need to discuss the 7 core ways that people learn:

Visual – Spatial. They prefer using pictures, images and spatial understanding
Aural – They prefer sound and music
Verbal – They prefer using words both in speech and writing
Solitary – They prefer to work alone
Social – They prefer to learn in groups or with other people
Logical – They prefer using logic, reasoning and systems
Physical – They prefer using their body hands and sense of touch

So you can certainly understand why sometimes you'll send an email and a parent will call you to explain exactly what you've written in an email or you'll be speaking with a parent at the office and they'll ask you to write what you said to them in an email. Knowing the learning styles helps you to understand that it's not that you've been ineffective in your communication or you've given the wrong message, it's just that the way you delivered that information was hard for the recipient to grasp.

Knowing this, it's easiest to break down the way humans learn things into 3 core methods:

- Auditory
- Visual
- Kinaesthetic

The listeners, the seeers and the feelers. I find this such a fascinating topic! This is not only great for communicating with your parents and students outside of the classroom, it's also great for inside the classroom. You know you've got a great teacher when they can demonstrate a step through showing, explaining with words then explaining how it should feel. Amazing!

Once you're aware of these three learning styles, you can really take it up a notch when communicating with your dance families. This is going to eliminate the multiple emails and phones calls asking you the same questions over and over again (I'm sure you know what I'm talking about!).

So what are the ways in which you can communicate with these different learning types effectively? Let's go through a few options...

Auditory

These people love hearing things. Live announcements in or after class, voicemail messages, voice recordings, phone conversations, audio messages on Facebook – anything to do with sound. Some private clients I work with now voice record their newsletters, upload it for free to Soundcloud and the response has been amazing. They also use Soundcloud now to make announcements and post them to their private studio Facebook groups. The auditory learners love this and it really doesn't take too much extra time to do. A lot less time than answering the same questions over and over!

Visual

These people love pictures, maps, images, diagrams, videos, signs and models. They love reading, visualizing and watching things. They will read the sign in the window of your office, look at the pictures on the newsletter and read your emails. They like pretty things, so be sure to include images alongside your text. Using models to explain things is another effective way to communicate to them and they also love watching live demonstrations to learn.

Kinaesthetic

These people love to touch and feel. They want something tangible. They love receiving your welcome pack with the pieces of paper, and they'll also want a printed version of your newsletter and any other notes you send out. They will also want to feel the material of the costumes.

So there you have it – the three different ways that people prefer to receive information. Most of us are a mix of all three, but prefer one way of learning over the other two.

Now, before you freak out and think I've just created a whole lot more work for you and the only way to stop all the questions is to start producing various forms of communication… take a deep breath, because I'm certainly not about creating more work for you. I'm about working smarter, more efficiently and more effectively – not harder.

Have you been to a musical theatre show? I'm sure you have. Think back to the days when you had to call up the ticketing company and your paper tickets were sent to you in the mail or collected from the box office. Now you can purchase tickets on an app on your smart phone and have the barcode scanned at the theatre from your phone. That has been a huge learning curve for many people, but the ticketing companies didn't ask us, the consumers, about their new method – they said this is how it works, so get used to it!

Now, I'm not saying that you have to take this direct and tough approach, but you can learn from it.

While you need to ensure you're hitting all the different learning styles with the important messages you need your studio families to know, things like newsletters are sent to email addresses or kept on a members only area of your website.

TIME FOR A COMMUNICATIONS AUDIT

The first thing you need to do is a communications audit. It's like that show Hoarders – before you know it you have a whole lot of stuff and you end up not being able to move! Make a list of all the ways you currently communicate to your students and parents: general announcements, concert and recital announcements, registration information, eisteddfod and festival announcements, fundraising information, timetable changes, costume information, rehearsal details. This process should take you an hour, and once that's done, go through all the communication you send out and see where you can cut down on paper. Generally, most studios can reduce printing costs by simply becoming effective at email. The thing with email communication is that you always need to ensure that the parents' details are up-to-date and the email address you have is the one they check.

I recently worked with a studio that was very paper heavy (notes every second week) and it was costing them a fortune, not to mention the notes rarely got to the parents. We went paperless with that school – for a three-week period, we sent out communication via email, post, on the Facebook group and through signs to say that the studio was going paperless and to update the email address at the office. They were slightly scared, but I knew this would save them heaps of time and money – not to mention prove way more effective! A month into the experiment and it's going great – they're using email and their private Facebook group to make announcements, and they've noticed that having only two places to view information has reduced email and phone calls as students and parents know where to look and check regularly. You'll be able to set up effective email lists in your dance business management system or your email system like SendPepper, as I mentioned previously.

So it's now time to make some decisions around how you'll start to effectively communicate in your studio moving forward. At the end of the day, your students and parents will adapt to what you decide. Don't be afraid to get more efficient and effective. Sure, you'll have a few parents saying they want the paper newsletter or the physical booklet with costume details, but you can tell them that you're saving the trees and email is the best way to give them up-to-date information.

TIME FOR A LITTLE FEEDBACK

I want to ask you a question... What do you think of when you hear the word feedback? Does your heart rate increase? Maybe you feel a little bit sick in the stomach? That's only natural. As human beings, there's certain feedback we love and certain feedback we don't... For example, you get ready for a romantic dinner with your partner and they say, 'Wow honey, you're a knock out! I'm so lucky to be with someone as amazing as you' – feedback we obviously like! But feedback that we're not so fond of? Say we meet someone we like for a first date, and they say, 'Sorry, I'm not interested. You're too old and definitely not my type.'

Feedback can hurt, but as a studio owner you need to continually be asking – and gracefully receiving – feedback from your students and their parents. Now before you skip this lesson, please hear me out. Over the last few years, many of my private clients have implemented feedback check points in to their calendar year so that they can ensure they're providing the best service possible. I mean, who wouldn't take a bit of pain for a lot of gain – and that's exactly what feedback does. Yes, it can sting, but at the end of the day, it helps us to grow our business.

So why should you be implementing a feedback strategy into your studio? Well, there are multiple reasons, so now let's run through the top six reasons you want to be grabbing feedback from your students and parents:

Referrals – If you're like most dance studios, a huge amount of your new student enquires would come from current student referrals. You don't want any reasons for a student or parent not to recommend your studio – I'm sure you want them to be raving fans. It's important that you check in to ensure there are no frustrations.

Loyalty – You never want to be surprised when a family leaves abruptly or doesn't come back for the following year. It's important that you find out any issues straight away so that they're faced with awesome customer service. You want to be the most responsive studio out there without being on call for all the small issues.

Retention – It's human nature for people to lie – so when you ask someone how they're finding things, they will likely say, 'Oh, just fine,' then go home and complain about that 'fine' thing to their family and friends. It's important that you make feedback really easy for them so they don't feel like it's awkward or that you'll blacklist them. Little niggles can build up over time… and when it builds up, it's a perfect time for a competing school to step in and grab them.

Student acquisition – Receiving feedback means you can publish it as testimonials on your website, social media and promotional material. This provides evidence that you're a great studio and will make new families more comfortable in coming to try a class with you.

Reputation – Feedback allows you to hear from your students and families first before they tell their friends. If it's great feedback then you can give them a high five and thank them; if it's not so good, then you can fix it before they go and tell the world. The important thing here is that there's an open door for them to give you the feedback and for you to respond with empathy and support, along with providing a solution.

Motivation – Have you ever had really glowing feedback that makes you so motivated and driven to do better? That happens. When we receive awesome feedback where people tell us that we're doing a good job, we want to really take it to the next level.

So now that we understand the awesome benefits of receiving feedback, let's talk about how you can generate the best results through receiving feedback. I'm not talking about how you can make the feedback all good, but how you can get the best feedback to assist you in providing the best service possible!

Gain clarity around your objectives – There are feedback forms that studio owners take notice of and make changes from that feedback, and there's feedback forms that go out because you should do them – but they ultimately end up in the bin because everyone is 'wrong'. If you're going to implement a feedback system, make sure you take them seriously and plan to pay attention to what people are saying – good and bad. I've seen feedback forms work against studios who don't take on any suggestions or speak with any of the parents, and then they think what they said is being ignored. This can backfire on you and you could end up losing students.

Make the feedback process easy and efficient – Have you ever been sent an email after you've purchased a product or service and it's about 20 questions long? Do you do it? Of course you don't, unless you've had a very bad experience. Make the feedback process at your studio really simple for your students and parents to participate in – multiple choice and plain text answers are best. Respect their time and instead of giving away a prize, assure them that their voice will be heard and action will be taken.

Develop relevant questions for your feedback forms – You want to make sure that your questions are short, sharp, to the point and most of all, relevant for them and you. We'll talk about more examples in a minute, but as an example, a question like 'Do you like your teacher?' could be replaced with, 'On a scale from 1-5, how inspiring, energetic and encouraging is your teacher, with 5 being the best outcome.'

Send your feedback form at the best time – Think about the events that your studio runs where you could ask for feedback afterwards – it could be at the end of the month or term, possibly after a concert or recital, or after exams. Sending surveys immediately after big events means that their thoughts are still fresh and they haven't had time to stew over any potential problems. You'll get their feedback straight.

Share feedback – It's important that your team are aware of the feedback that has come in. Celebrate the wins and take the lessons from the not-so-positive feedback. This process is about everyone growing and learning.

Evaluate Your Feedback Strategy – As with every aspect of your business, you need to evaluate if this process is providing you with the best results. Ask yourself:

- Is student and parent satisfaction improving?
- Are you increasing student retention?
- Are you receiving great comments and displaying them on your website, on social media and in promotional materials?
- Is your team's customer service issues reducing?

So what are the types of feedback forms you can implement in your studio?

- New enrollment feedback form
- Exit survey
- Teacher feedback from students and parents
- Studio feedback from students and parents
- Studio feedback from Teachers
- Regular feedback form

That completes our Feedback Frenzy! I hope you've received awesome tips on implementing a feedback strategy into your studio.

YOU WILL HAVE UNHAPPY CUSTOMERS

No matter how hard we try to please everyone, we're going to have unhappy customers. In this chapter, I'll walk you through how to manage these sticky situations to ensure your reputation stays intact and that there is minimal impact on the studio.

Let's be really honest for a moment. Over the years I've worked with many clients who I like to describe as 'people pleasers,' and unfortunately dance studio owners take the lead in this space because they are passionate about their business and have huge hearts. No matter how large or small your studio is, you're always going to have a percentage of students and parents who won't smell the roses. I'm sure you've already started picturing these parents. We all have customers who are never happy and always want us to change the rules for them. You know the type of parent I'm talking about.... The one who thinks it's unfair that their child is not in the front row, the parent who thinks you're playing favorites, the parent who says a teacher spoke inappropriately to their child, the one who says your costumes are too expensive and that you're greedy and finally, the parent who doesn't think they need to pay their fees when everyone else does.

Now, in saying all of this, sometimes complaints are warranted and you should listen to them and take action! We spoke about surveys, which will greatly help you in this space, but here I wanted to share with you the six effective ways in managing complaints and dissatisfaction.

6 Ways To Manage Complaints & Dissatisfaction

1. Take ownership – None of us are perfect and yes, we all make mistakes. This is no different for you in your business. But I don't like to call them mistakes; I like to call them lessons, and rather than point the finger and place blame on others, the buck stops with you. As a studio owner, if a teacher is not performing or an unpopular decision has been made, you need to take responsibility and then address the issue. The key point here is to learn the lesson quickly – then move on.

2. Remove emotion – For students and parents, there's a lot of emotion that comes with the experience of learning how to dance. When a parent or student is coming to you with a complaint, it's often reactive

to something that has just happened or happened in class over the last 24 hours, and is supercharged with emotions. Rarely will a parent or student look at the situation subjectively, put themselves in your shoes and try to understand why a decision was made as an example. So let's say that you receive an angry email or phone call from a parent – your initial response would be to take it personally and be reactive in your response, which means you most probably will say something you'll regret. I want you to be empathetic. Put yourself in their shoes to understand as much as you can about what they're feeling. At the end of the day, it generally has nothing to do with you and is about them. Breathe and have a calm conversation.

3. Be professional – It's a fact that students will come and go from your studio. Some may have been at your studio for years and then decided to try somewhere else or go to another activity after school. I remember once attending a studio where the owner was saying very nasty things about a student who had left. They were telling other parents all the work they had put into this student and they just packed up and went to another studio. There was so much resentment for this family and while I showed empathy, I also had a conversation with her about being so attached to students. At the end of the day, they are your customers. A customer pays you for a product or service, you deliver what they purchased, and sometimes they will come back for more – sometimes they won't. While I love the culture and support a dance studio can ingrain into their dance families, it's important that as a studio owner you keep your space and know that at the end of the day, you're running a business. Period.

4. Learn to love feedback – Let down your defenses, be open and coachable when it comes to receiving feedback. I totally get that you've invested probably a large chunk of your life to your studio, so when someone says or writes something unfavorable, you'll want to fight back. This studio is like your baby. Again, as much as it hurts to hear, there will occasionally be some truth to what is being said. I know some people are just plain crazy, but the bottom line is we all have a voice and we should all be heard. I encourage you to listen carefully to all types of feedback. Just take it on board, take on board what you want and do

away with the rest. As I mentioned throughout this book, you always want to be improving, right? Being open to feedback will help with that improvement.

5. Have a Wisdom Circle – We all need those rocks in our life, who we can turn to when things get a little tougher than expected. You know when we have a challenging night teaching or start to feel overwhelmed as the concert or recital looms? Surrounding yourself with 3-5 people in a supportive network is crucial for anyone, not just studio owners. I created the concept of the wisdom circle a few years ago after selling my second business DanceLife. I've continued to implement having a group of supportive people in my wisdom circle now, and each of them support me in different ways. Let me ask you, have you ever gone to your partner to speak with them about something that's happening at the studio which has upset you, and they cannot for the life of them understand why you're upset? They may say something like, 'Why are you so worked up? Just move on…. It's not a big deal.' Does that sound familiar? And do you continue to go to them with the same issues, only to get more and more frustrated with them? I liken this to going to your local Chinese restaurant and asking for Nachos. You don't go to Chinese expecting to be able to get Nachos, so why do you continually go to your partner wanting empathy and compassion when you know you're not going to get it? Accept this and find someone else you can get that from. These people make up your wisdom circle. For instance, in my wisdom circle I have five – two mentors, two friends and my mum. Each of them complement each other, yet I'm supported on different levels from each. It's one of the best things I ever did in my life and I encourage you to do the same.

6. Be strong – When dealing with a concern or problem, many studio owners either give the parent or student what they want or make them even angrier that they tell all the other parents about it and could end up leaving. It's important as a studio owner that you remain firm and fair. You cannot treat one person's feedback differently to another person's – they are all paying customers and you need to treat their thoughts as equally as possible. In saying that, it's important you stay firm on your policies. I see too many studio owners bend the rules

for particular students and parents because they're afraid of a student leaving. I always say to my private clients, if your teachers are fantastic, your business systems are fantastic, then a minor concern or problem from a parent or student won't make them leave.

People Will Come & Go

What I want you to remember, and what I say over and over again to my clients, is that you can't be all things to all people. During the life of your studio, people will come and go, but your focus will always be on building the business – ensure it's creating a great impact on the lives of your students and dance families and is providing you with a great income.

Now, I've spoken a lot about parents and students here, but the six things I've just spoken about also apply to your teachers and staff. As I've mentioned in previous chapters, your faculty are the backbone to your business and you need to give them the same eyes and ears as you do for your customers.

Proper or Pretend Problem?

So I guess the question now is… how do you know how to distinguish between a proper problem and a pretend problem? You see, as studio owners, we are faced with people coming to us with problems, but if we kept a tally of all of these I'm sure you'd see that 90% of them can be fixed in a second and are pretend problems, while others have more weight and merit and therefore need your attention.

For example, you are losing students from tap and you've had a few people mention that the class is boring. That there is a proper problem and you need to find a new tap teacher.

Another proper problem is when you notice that fees are not coming in as regularly as they used to, and when you approach people about paying, they complain about how rude your office staff are and are never accommodating. This is a proper problem and you need to address it.

One more example happening more and more often is bullying on social media. This is a problem that is prevalent in schools and is also transferring to studios. If your teachers are noticing a divide between students and parents have started to talk, then this is a proper problem and needs to be addressed immediately.

As a studio owner, it's your responsibility to know when problems become proper problems. Get in there and provide solutions quickly to limit any damage that might affect your studio.

3 Steps To Addressing Concerns

So I've given you the tools to add to your tool belt when it comes to managing complaints and dissatisfaction but I wanted to give you one last nugget which I used when I owned my studio which I now pass on to all my private mentoring clients. It's a simple 3 step process to addressing concerns.

1. Thank them – Straight up, we want to thank them for being honest and transparent with you and coming directly to you with their concern.

2. State your commitment and intention – It's then important that you state your commitment. For instance, 'Mrs Smith, I'm committed to providing our students with a high quality of dance training while ensuring they having an enjoyable experience at each and every lesson.' Then when you state your intention, you want to make this relevant to the situation. As an example, 'Mrs Smith, my intention was never to make you angry or upset, my intention was to ensure we implemented a policy that applied to all students.'

3. Ask them - You then want to ask them what they would have done differently and then say that you've certainly taken what they've said on board and that you'll take the appropriate action.

Be Accessible – Open Door Policy

I'm sure you've heard all about the open door policy before. You hear it flung around in large corporate organizations all the time. At the core, having an open door policy is about being accessible, allowing easy flow of communication and to maintain closer relationships with your staff, parents and students – without being their close friends.

So the question then is about how you have an open door policy that doesn't run your life, but allows your customers and staff to feel comfortable talking with you about their thoughts and concerns. Many studio owners ask me why they should have an open-door policy. Here are the 3 benefits of opening your door:

1. Laser beam access – It's important that your studio family can feel comfortable coming to you and sharing their concerns when an important issue arises, rather than brew on the issue and make it even bigger! By not having an open door when it comes to people sharing their immediate concerns, and on the flip side, creative ideas on how you could improve your studio, you'll become disengaged which will result in your students' numbers going down, down, down.

2. On the pulse – Do you really know what's happening inside and outside of your studio in regards to students, parents and teachers? Being accessible allows you to keep on top of the latest news from inside the classes and beyond. Your staff will be more engaged and you will see your student retention rates rise.

3. Be active – The culture of your studio comes from you and then filters down through your teachers, students and parents. An open-door policy builds a belief in others that the studio owner really wants to be actively engaged with daily activities. I'm not saying that you need to be across everything all of the time but be interested and occasionally go in and get your hands dirty! If you have a closed door most of the time, your teachers and dance families could sense a feeling of secretiveness, which can negatively affect relationships with your staff and customers.

Can you see the benefits of an open-door policy? Now, let's discuss how you can implement a keep in touch strategy that will keep you in the loop without taking on more work, while ensuring all your staff and parents feel supported and listened to.

Drop into classes – It's really special for the students and the teacher when a studio owner drops in unannounced to watch part of a class. Sure, the teacher will freak out slightly at first, but then they'll love the fact that you're showing interest in their class and what they're doing. Tell the students how much of a great job they're doing and provide the teacher with some positive feedback on their class and teaching style. You should be dropping into classes at least once a month. When I was teaching, I would feel really special when the studio owner would drop in and be passionate about my work as a teacher.

Don't show stress – When I go and do work with studio owners on site, quite often I will just observe their studio over a few days, and one thing I see often is the studio owner running around like a chook with their head cut off ready to snap at anyone who utters their name. I know you're busy, but you can be busy and pleasant, energetic and friendly, or you can be busy and bitter. You select how you are in the presence of your customers and teachers. Busy is a given, so move on from that and focus on providing out-of-this-world customer service.

Make regular communication times – At times, a parent or student will want to speak with you via phone outside of studio hours. Some studio owners I've worked with in the past have a strict rule around this and won't talk to anyone outside of the time they're in the studio, but personally, I encourage all my clients to have a 1-2 hour block each week that is dedicated for calls requested by students or parents. It may be a Wednesday morning for a few hours as an email. You can use an online schedule booking system like Set More or TimeTrade so they can book in the phone chat themselves and you just sit down with a cup of tea or coffee and do the calls. I've seen this approach boost retention and create a really satisfied group of parents, students and teachers. It's awesome!

Love and support cannot be bought – All human beings have the desire to feel loved, supported and to feel a sense of belonging. These things cannot be bought, but as a studio owner you can certainly provide these qualities to your families and teachers. The important thing here is to maintain being the supportive studio owner and not slip into becoming everyone's best friend. Create an environment where people are part of a family. As we know, all families have their problems, but if you really listen and maintain the respect of your studio families you'll see a complete shift, meaning that your retention will increase and so will your referrals. Plus, as a studio owner, don't you want to walk into a joyful studio as opposed to one where people are complaining and gossiping all the time?

ENGAGE STUDENTS OUTSIDE OF THE CLASSROOM

By now you would have a Facebook page for your studio which is awesome, but how can the types of things you post on Facebook really get your students and current dance families engaged outside of the class room? We'll tackle that topic now.

You see, as more and more of our customers are using social media, the more we need to know and embrace it because I'm telling you now that it's sticking around! I'm sorry, but the days of only communicating through printed letters is history, so buckle up your seat belt and let's take this social media Mercedes for a drive.

Some of you may be asking, 'Shouldn't my energy be on acquiring new students through social media?' My answer is of course you should be spending time on this, but considering it costs you five times more to acquire a new student than to retain an existing student, I always want to focus on the people you're currently serving.

Increase Retention & Communicate Efficiently

Having a closed Facebook group is the first big way you can use social media to increase retention, but also drive down the ways in which people communicate with you. Universities have been using these private groups to encourage more conversation outside of the classroom and they have seen class attendance rates rise as well as students accelerating the getting to know you process; this is then transferring to real-life relationships in the classroom and around campus.

At this very moment, you're either thinking one of two things. Believe me, I've worked with enough studio owners over the years to know what your initial reaction is to creating a private Facebook group. Number one – you immediately think of all those problem parents and students who will post negative things about the studio on it and want to cause trouble, or number two – you can see the immediate value of implementing this to really build your studios community offline which in turn will increase loads of things including retention, referrals, happiness and your reputation.

I can tell you right now that I've never had any clients say they've had people write horrible things in the group. And if you're going to tell me that your parents and students are different, hold off as I've heard it all before – and even they have made this work. I'm certainly not here to make your life harder – that's not why you're here, so please trust me on this one. I've seen one simple thing – that will take you less than five minutes to set up on Facebook – that can really transform the culture and the way people communicate in the studio. Oh, and don't freak out either – you will only need to spend 2 x 10 minute blocks per day on the group as a lot of the time other students or parents will jump in if they can help. Once in the morning and once before classes start in the afternoon. I want you to remember though that this group is different to your page, where you are building awareness of your studio with potential new students.

Your Closed Facebook Group

To create your closed Facebook group, simply type into the Facebook tool bar up the top create a group, click on it and follow the prompts. You can then make the group closed, which means you can send the link to people then approve them, or secret, which means you'll need to have them as a friend and invite them.

Closed is much easier to facilitate. You can then send all your studio families an email that tells them how excited you are to be launching the closed Facebook group with the link to join the group. Your students and parents will absolutely love this. When you send out the email ensure you have a few guidelines but most of all let them know the benefits they'll receive, like knowing up to date information, being able to network with all studio families, being able to see what's happening at the studio each week and what you have coming up. It's like a continual newsletter for them.

So let's talk about the super-cool content you can post in your group to increase engagement and retention. Every dance studio owner is different in terms of what they are comfortable posting and not, so I'll just give you all the ideas I've seen really work and you can create a pick and mix bag of things you'd like to implement.

Super Engaging Content

1. New teachers – You might have a new teacher starting at the studio. Make sure you make a party out of it and post cool photos or videos of the teacher along with the great things they've been doing in their career.

2. Costumes – Maybe you've been sketching some cool new costumes for a performance group. Take a photo of a sketch and see if they can guess what dance and age group the costume is for.

3. Notices – You may need to get something out there quite quickly that relates to a class that day or the next. This is a great platform to put short and sharp messages. Don't worry that not everything you post will be for everyone - they won't mind at all. In fact they will love knowing what's going on and appreciate your transparency. Just start the post with Attention Level 2 Jazz, for example.

4. Say congratulations – You might have had some students perform really well at a competition or festival, and you want to say a big congratulations. Post up a photo and say how proud you are.

5. Events – Maybe you have a crazy hair day at the studio or watching week is coming up. You can post a reminder and promote these events easily on the group.

6. Ask questions – Now this one can scare a few people, but people love giving their opinions. I'm not talking about asking something like, 'Do you think we should increase our classes by $1?' I'm talking about… 'Attention Open Commercial Jazz – I'm loving these two songs at the moment. Which one would you love to dance to this week?'

7. Personal insights – At the end of the day, people buy you; you are the studio owner and while some studio owners like to keep their personal life completely private, I think it's important that your studio families get to have a peek inside your world as a normal human being. Maybe just a picture once every few weeks of you and your partner out to dinner, or a candid snap during a family day out. It's important that they see you as a real person too!

8. Competitions – It may be coming up to Easter, so you might do a colouring in competition for your junior students, where you post the picture for them to download and colour in and bring it into the studio. I'm going to show you how to create competitions that drive referrals through your currents students in our next module.

9. Special offers – You might be launching a new uniform piece and have a special offer on it, or maybe you might offer all current students

the opportunity to try any class they like that week for free. Promote the different offers you have for your studio.

Encourage your dance studio families to populate the group with photos from competitions, practicing at home (maybe the splits!). It's always great to get them building the page for you as well!

10. Educate your families – I love this one. You have multiple classes running each week and it's probably true that not all your families know exactly all of the services you offer, so this group is a great place to talk about the cool other things you offer in the studio. Sure, they might have heard someone talking about the musical theatre class, but no one has ever explained how it works.

When it comes to how often you're posting content on the group, I suggest you do this during your 2 x 10 minute sessions on the group. This closed Facebook group strategy in itself can turn around your retention results.

Take It To The Next Level

I'm about to give you a bonus tip, which would be awesome for you to implement into your studio. But I'd love you to take it one step further and measure the results.

Let's run through the core elements I want you to track:

1. Increased retention rate – This is hard to track in a month, but in six months, you compare it to the same six months as last year and see how you rate. I'm positive that you'll see an increase!

2. Decreased phone calls and text messages – By implementing the group, have you received less phone calls and text messages from parents, students and teachers because they are finding the information in the group?

3. Student saves – How many students were going to drop out but because of their engagement with your group, you've managed to hold onto them and turn them into a raving fan?

4. Improved systems and processes – How many systems and processes have you been able to improve thanks to the feedback that you've been able to get straight away from your customers? Think about how much time and money this will save you in the long run!

5. Cross-class sell – Have you been able to enroll your current studios into other classes through your posts on your group?

6. Complaints turned into raves – You may have a parent or student who puts a complaint on the page. Instead of deleting it, address it. We spoke about how to deal with a complaint in our communications chapter – do the same if you receive it on your group or event your page. When they get a response quickly, see how fast their complaint turns into them recommending you due to the way you handle the situation.

Ready To Launch?

Are you now ready to launch your closed Facebook group? If you already have a group, are you ready to start using it to its full potential? I know this strategy alone will change the way communication flows in your studio, plus you'll keep more of your students.

YOU'RE NOT JUST GIVING DANCE CLASSES

I believe education is one of the most valuable things we have in this world. Education grows us not only as business owners but as human beings. I love this quote by Mahatma Gandhi: 'Live as if you were to die tomorrow. Learn as if you were to live forever.' I love learning and I truly believe that as a studio owner, you need to be continually on a journey of growth – both creatively and on the business side of things. That's why it was important for me to talk about how you can make a greater impact on your students, staff and dance families, through not only teaching them how to dance, but how to teach them to find purpose in their life and simply be amazing human beings.

I remember speaking recently with a mother whose child was doing dance class. She told me that her daughter was not a natural dancer, yet she took her there not to become a professional performer, but to learn life skills such as resilience, courage, confidence and acceptance. You see, the mother believed that these attributes would make her daughter the shining individual that she knew she could be. This child started classes a few years back as a very, very shy little girl, who had limited confidence. The parent admitted that it wasn't easy getting her to class for the first two months, but one day, she collected her daughter from class and she said, 'Mummy, I love my dancing.' From that moment, the mother saw her daughter slowly but surely become more and more herself, doing the things that made her happy and not the things she thought everyone else wanted her to do.

At the heart of a dance class, this is what we're teaching. We're teaching a child to simply be themselves. We're teaching that no matter what other people say or the way they act towards you, be yourself.

As I write this, I feel this is a big introduction into this topic, but I'm just so passionate about the life skills that being a part of a dance studio can provide people with.

To ensure your students keep coming back each and every year, it's important to continually take the education aspect of your studio to the next level, from attending professional shows and company works to putting your teachers and staff through training, which we've spoken about. Education filters from the top down, meaning more reasons for your existing students to stay. In this chapter, I'll explore the key ways to educate and inspire your tribe to ensure motivation and inspiration continues for years to come.

How To Educate And Inspire

I started dancing when I was nine and teaching when I was 14 as a student teacher, and I still remember those teachers who greatly impacted my life. Without a doubt, they shaped me to be the person I am today. Let me share with you what you and your teachers can be doing in the classroom to educate and inspire your students to ensure you're not only producing talented performers, but extraordinary human beings.

1. Visualizations – Do you have a vision board? I do. And to be honest with you, many big successes in my life to date started on a vision board – hence why I believe so strongly in them. When teaching classes leading up to the concert or a big competition, or maybe it's a senior group of students who are leaving you, I love getting everyone on the floor, lying down with their heads to the sky, turning off the lights, putting on some instrumental music

and getting them to visualize every part of that experience. If you're doing this with a group who are training to have a full-time career in the industry, then talk them through this. Maybe it's the process of them going to dance for Beyonce on tour – I'd even finish this exercise by playing "Crazy In Love" and ask them to picture themselves dancing with Queen Bey on opening night. Start getting them in a success mindset; that if they do the work they will achieve anything. Also encourage them to spend at least 2 x 30 minute sessions a week to visualize.

2. Give homework – I'm not talking about the boring work they get in school – I'm talking uber creative and exciting homework that will get them closer to reaching their goals, along with becoming an outstanding performer and person. Every month or every second month, get them to do an assignment for you that is going to help them grow. Here are some great examples for your students:

Reach out and ask to interview a performer that you admire. This is a funny one because so many people are afraid to reach out, but the truth is that no one is doing it. There are plenty of talented dancers and performers in the world who are making an amazing career from doing what they love each and every day – the assignment I would give is to ask them for an hour of their time, prepare your questions and Skype them or meet in person if you can. Ask them questions about their journey and the keys to their success. Then after the interview, I tell them to write a one-page article about the wisdom they received from the person.

3. Make a film clip – These days, it's important that performers also have a great understanding of technology. I know plenty of performers who have filmed and edited their own showreels and they look amazing. Not only do your students need to be triple threats they also need to be a triple threat when it comes to technology – Film, Edit, Deliver.

4. Write a journal – In my opinion, reflecting on your day is an important part of your growth as a human being. It's great to ask your students to keep a journal for 30 days. It doesn't need to be long, but I would ask them at the end of each day to write down the three things they accomplished that day and one lesson they learned. Leave this up to each child to

interpret; I don't like to put too many guidelines around this one. The exercise will start shifting their mindset to start looking for the good instead of the bad. They will be actively patting themselves on the back to say, 'Hey, good job today. Now what did I learn today?' This is not just homework for your students, I'd say it's homework for you too!

5. Study a legend – This is similar to the task I mentioned on point one, but I'm not sure if you could pick up the phone to Fred Astaire and say, 'Hi, can I spend an hour with you over Skype?' I ask the students to write a one or two-page article that outlines their career to date, which is essentially a timeline of that person's life so far. Now, it's easy to Google and get a timeline straight up, but I encourage them to do further research and under each of the new entries in the timeline, write the one thing they might have done or did to get them to that next stage. It helps your students to start thinking about progression and how to get from one point to another.

Create your timeline – Based on the last exercise, the other thing I like to get them to do is to create their own timeline of their life, from where they are now to where they want to be. For example, if they're 15 years old, I ask them where they want to be at the age of 35. Then I'll ask what they want to be doing each year until then. Again, this is another way of visualizing, but it also starts to put in place a plan for them, one which they can change and alter as they go along. So many students might say they want to be in a musical on Broadway which is awesome – I love hearing that – but after commending them on their dream, I ask how they plan to get there. This timeline will help them gain some clarity.

There you have my five homework tasks. I know how well these tasks have served studio owners when they've implemented them into their studio, and I hope it will do the same for you.

RETENTION IS THE OUTCOME, NOT THE GOAL

The goal is to build better human beings and I strongly believe that by gaining clarity on your class objectives and providing your students with valuable lessons they can take away, your studio will reach a completely new level.

Get Your Attention On Retention

As we've discussed, there are many ways to keep your students happy, learning and growing at your studio. From social events to in-house promotions, there is something that your studio could be doing right now that it may not be doing. Let's start raising the retention across your studio with some proven strategies that will increase the overall fulfilment for you, your teachers and your students.

When I first sit down with our program members, I ask them what their retention rates are for their studio year on year, and about 90% of them cannot tell me. The funny thing is, though, that the ones who don't know, estimate that it's very good – about 80-90% – but when we dig into the figures, it usually sits more around 55-70%. As studio owners, we know that what we do makes a big difference in the lives of our students and dance families who stay, but we quickly forget the ones that come for just a class or two and never again. This is the problem. I love the numbers, as you know, and if you're not tracking retention on your weekly report, then you're not really in the loop of what's happening in your business.

One important facet of calculating your retention rate is to do it by the year, not by the term or month. You see, if you're just calculating it in these short bursts, you won't get a true representation of what your retention rate really is.

The reason you need to know your retention rates is to:

a) plan for how many new students you need to recruit per year to maintain your numbers, and more importantly
b) ascertain how many new students you need to enroll for you to reach your goals relating to student numbers.

Retention is our final chapter, as if you've put into place excellent business and procedures, and have passionate and dedicated teachers with engaging class structures, then that will automatically bump up your retention. To lift your retention rates even further, let me share with you the things you can be doing to keep your students loving your studio.

Activating Past Students

Firstly, I want to talk about your past students. You know, the ones who have left you to go off somewhere else, maybe to a sport and occasionally to another dance studio. By now you would have implemented your exit survey, so you'll have an idea of why they left. But after they have been gone for three months, I like to send them a 'We Miss You' postcard by direct mail – not an email, but a postcard that goes to their mailbox. You'll be able to run this report on your dance studio software and then have your office staff member send them out. Get them printed and ensure you include an offer. In regards to the copy of the postcard, you might have 'We Miss You' with a strong image, and on the back, a short, handwritten note and an offer to come back and spend a week with the studio. Sure, they left for a reason so I also like to include on the back:

Dear Sally, we've missed seeing your smiling face here at Jazz Hands Studio. We've made some changes since you were last with us and I'd love to invite you back for a week's worth of classes, on me. Simply call or email us within the next seven days to arrange your week. Look forward to seeing you, Clint.

I also include an expiry so that they take action straight away. Another tip? Make sure you have mentioned that they can pass this offer on to a friend or family member – it's this line that will guarantee it won't end up in the bin. After this, simply keep them on your newsletter.

Now, what about all those students who enquired about your classes but never came? When you follow the enrollment process in module 4 you'll call them a few times before you simply add them to your newsletter and hope that keeps them keen. In some cases, you'll get their enrollment from that, but you know me well enough by now to know that I never like to leave anything to chance. With your non-enrollers, three months down the track I want you to send them an email as we went through with the auto responder emails. In the marketing world, it's called the nine-word email. This email should read along these lines:

Hi Sally,

Just wondering if you're still interested in dance classes?

Warm regards
Clint

It's remarkable the amount of people that reply to these emails. Real estate agents use these all the time and they have proven to be highly effective, and many studio owners have implemented this strategy and seen a great response. Some people will not write back, some will say they're not interested and some will say yes. Even if one person a month says yes, and all you've done is set up an automated email sequence, that's a good result.

Caught Them, Now Learn How To Keep Them

Now comes the super fun part. Once you have your students through the door, how can you keep them there? Well, you need to provide them with awesome training, teachers and run a super-slick organized business, but I now want to walk you through the 12 top retention strategies that you can set up in your studio.

1. Monthly goals – When a student enrolls in your classes at the studio, it's important you find out why they're signing up. Sure, if they're three years old, then it's their parents' decision, not theirs. So why did their parent enroll them in dance classes?

As the students get older, I encourage the studio owner to get each of their students to send in their goal for the month, at the beginning of every month. Now you may have over 1000 students, the idea here is not to reply to them, but for them to know that you have them. It's an accountability thing and during the month they need to work hard to reach their goal. What I love about this is that sometimes it's not even about class – it's about losing weight and becoming healthier or to help their mum more around the house. Then when they see you they might say, 'Hey Mr Clint, I can do a double pirouette already and it's only two weeks into the month.' This is what makes you smile – students growing and learning.

2. Your studio book – I didn't mention this in the enrollment process as I like this to come two weeks after a new student has started class. It's a branded book with your studio logo on it where your students can track their goals, things to practice, important notes given out in class and really, anything that is happening at the studio. The idea is that they use it for the year and then the following year, they purchase a book from the studio which then becomes another source of income for you. I've worked with some clients who have created an app that does the same thing. However, there's something about a book that the students love. It's tangible and they can be really creative with what goes inside.

3. Dance exams – Some studios offer exams and some don't. I'm all for teaching syllabus work in your studio, as it provides students with an excellent technical foundation – the same way you're doing this training process. A syllabus acts like building blocks, where in each lesson, your students can see progression. This is important. I've found over the last few years working with studio owners that there are more drop outs in the open classes than exam classes – and it's because there's no real structure and the students don't feel like they're achieving. Even if you don't do exams, offering syllabus work at your studio will certainly increase your retention.

4. A pathway – If you think about an employee who goes to work in an organization, they're more keen to take a position where there is room to grow and move up in the company. This is not too different in a dance studio. The same way I spoke about how syllabus work provides progression for the students, it's important there is a plan in place for them. Maybe it's that they want to move on to be a student teacher – how does that work for them? Maybe they want to start auditioning for shows – how can you help them with that? It's important to be having these conversations with your students, especially the teenage ones.

5. Looking forward to events – You know when you decide to book a holiday in two months' time, how excited you get in the lead up to that holiday? Well, I want you to think about introducing events into your studio that do the same things for your students. Events like your concerts or recitals, competitions and workshops are perfect to put on the calendar to get your students excited.

6. Create a social studio – When your students are juniors you don't have too much competition; basically, if they're not at dance class, then they're at home. But as they get older, they have more options, more distractions and more things they could be doing besides being at dance class. As I've mentioned, the main thing all humans need is to be connected to other human beings, so why not create more of a social scene at your studio? Can you afford to have a timetable that creates small gaps between classes where your students can interact? I also suggest that at least four times per year, you organise studio social events like a disco, or picnic, maybe even go and see a show with everyone. I don't expect you to be spending all your free time mixing with your customers, but four times a year is nice – and easily doable.

7. Studio uniform – This one may sound a little odd to you, but do you know the amount of students who won't return to dance class because they feel uncomfortable in your studio uniform? If you only allow a leotard, then think about having additional clothing items that can cater for all shapes and sizes. It would be disappointing to have students leaving you because they feel self-conscious. Think about this – why do some people not go to the beach? Because they don't want to be seen in a swimsuit.

8. Celebrate birthdays – I'm a big fan of sending birthday cards out in the mail, which I know can take some time, but I believe is totally worth it. I've worked with many studio owners who have had their own studio cards made and send them out each month. Alternatively, you can have a poster made that you email out and personalize for each of your students. The other option is with your junior school to pick a new birthday song each year, and in the last two minutes of class if you have any birthdays for the week, you play the song, everyone in the class sings and you make a circle and dance around the birthday students. The students love this one!!

9. Pick up the phone – Most studio owners cringe when I say pick up the phone, but hear me out. Now you know that there are parents in your studio who come in most weeks to say hello and chat with other parents, and then there are some who you never see. Those are the ones

I'm talking about here. If you're not seeing some students parents, it's important they receive a call from you or staff member every 90 days to check in, say hello and see how their child is going with classes. I have seen this hands-down boost student retention rates.

10. In class competitions – Each month or term, it's a good idea to once again think about the progression of your students. You might like to introduce a fun, friendly competition. For example, who can increase the amount of pirouettes they can do or decrease the amount of inches they are from the floor when doing the splits. You can do different competitions for each class, and keep a chart to see the progression and results people are getting.

11. Celebrate their anniversaries – 5 and 10 year appreciation awards are a really great initiative to introduce into your studio. These are awards for the students who have been at your studio for 5 or 10 years. You could have a dinner all together, acknowledge them at the end of your concert or recital, or organize a half or full day trip out to see a show. It's important that you make a bit of a fuss over these people; they've been a big part of your studio.

12. Performance opportunities – I touched on creating events in the calendar to get your students excited, and to expand on that, performance opportunities are really exciting for your students. It gives them an opportunity to get out there and be seen while showcasing what they've been working on. It's obviously a great way for you to promote the studio as well. Think about local school events, Easter shows or Christmas shows – lots of events are seasonal, so it's a great idea to make a list of the events you could be involved in and contact the event organizer well in advance to see if you can be involved. Then, ensure it goes on your calendar so your students can get excited about it!

The first thing I would love you to do is work out your true retention rate, and then you can start working on implementing these strategies into your studio. Pick 2-4 strategies that you'll implement over the next six months, then schedule in the others.

I'm a big lover of retention and really delivering beyond expectations, so I hope I've injected some of my passion in this area over to you if you needed it. Most studio owners I meet are as passionate about retention as me and just need the tools to make it work. Now you have those tools!

We have covered a lot of ground in Dance Studio Transformation. Chapter 12 is all about your next steps and how you can truly grow your business, improve your quality of life as a studio owner, and impact the lives or more people. Turn the page and let the journey continue!

Chapter Twelve

YOUR NEXT BEST MOVE

'All our dreams can come true if we have the courage to pursue them.' ~ Walt Disney

Congratulations, you made it! You're in a very small percentage of people who purchased this book and actually made it the whole way through. I'm proud of you and you should be proud of yourself for making it this far.

When writing this book, my aim was to give you some philosophy, some strategy and a bunch of tactics so that you would gain the tools you need to transform your studio. I also arranged this as a guide that you can revisit time and time again, and just like our programs, I know that every time you go back through a particular chapter or section of the book that you'll see something you didn't the first time – and that could be the very thing that catapults your studio to the next level.

One thing I've noticed over and over again in this industry is that so many studio owners see owning a dance studio as a jail sentence. Once you're in, you can't get out. You can't have freedom, you can't have dinner with your family each night, you can't enjoy free time even when your business is running smoothly. But I'm hoping that by going through this book, I've opened your eyes to the opportunity that lies in front of you.

No matter where you're at currently in your studio, there is an exciting new step for you to reach – and that's just the beginning. I want you to grow your business, increase your profits and the impact you're making on your community by serving more people, but I also want you to get more from your life. I want your joy and fulfilment levels to rise.

In Chapter 1 we clearly defined where you are in your studio currently, but more importantly, where you want to go. It's so important that you look at your goals every day to ensure you're staying on track, and it's also great to have them near you during the day. I have mine above my laptop – to keep me accountable and to check that the work I'm doing at the moment is helping me move closer to my goals.

Once you have those goals in place, you can use all the strategies and tactics I mention in the book to get you there. My advice is to have a plan, execute the plan and then assess the plan. This is the process that is going to see each area of your studio thrive. It's certainly not rocket science, but it will require you to take disciplined action and not to waver off course and chase other opportunities along the way. Sure, be flexible with your plan, but don't bounce from one shiny object to another.

As we wind up our time together, you may be thinking a couple of things…

a) I've gone through the book, but I'm finding it a challenge to actually put these strategies and tactics into place. I need help with being held accountable to do the work.

b) I've really enjoyed the book and going through the exercises, but how do I get help implementing the systems and creating the step-by-step action plan to move forward?

c) I've implemented the ideas in the book and I'm ready for more advanced systems, strategies and the tactics to grow my dance studio.

If you're in any of these camps, then I have some great news for you. I'd love to invite you to look into joining Studio Success Formula, our most popular business growth training program for dance studio owners. It's a 12-week online program that walks you through how you can take your studio to the next level and beyond... plus you get support from me and my team to ensure you get there!

To find out more about the program, please visit www.studiosuccessformula.com or email transform@studiosuccessformula.com with any questions you have.

Again, I want to thank you for joining me on this journey to transforming your dance studio – and I hope we get the opportunity to work together on a deeper level inside our program.

To your success!

Clint

ACKNOWLEDGEMENTS

If you had told me when I was nine years old and first started dancing that I would go on to coach thousands of studio owners across the globe on how to grow their business and write a book about it at the age of 30, I wouldn't have believed you. But today, I couldn't imagine doing anything else. More importantly, I couldn't imagine making this journey without the people who have helped me over the last 14 years, since starting my first studio. It is these people who have made this book, and the life I lead today, truly possible.

Those people are:

My first dance teacher, Kristine Haines-Kellner, who took me under her wing, encouraged me and mentored me from being a dancer to a dance teacher.

Kelly-Lee Darby, who I started the dance studio with at 16, a studio that we ran together for five years. Without you, there would have been no studio and as I look back on our time together, I'm so grateful for that journey we went on – even in those challenging times!

Lauren Miller from the Harry M Miller Group. I've never worked with an organization where I learned so much in an environment where I really got to figure out who I was, and what I really wanted from life. I'll never forget my time at HMMG.

Nikita, who has been my friend since primary school and edited this book. Not only do I value our friendship, but I'm in awe of your out-of-this-world writing skills. Thank you for taking on this project that I'm so passionate about, and for handling it with care.

The people who have impacted my journey to date are no longer a part of my life. I'm grateful for the time we had together and the lessons you taught me.

To all the mentors who have coached me from near and far over the past years, my life and business would not be where it is today without you! Ryan Levesque, Todd Herman, Devin & Melanie Duncan, Amy Porterfield, Nathan Latka, Dan Martell, Noah Kagan, Lewis Howes, Marie Forleo, Matt Church, Terry Hawkins, Robert Michon, Michael Port, Darren Hardy, Chris Ducker, Barbara Corcoran, Tim Ferriss, Rory Vaden, Christina Guidotti, Jayson Gaignard, Emma Isaacs, Ali Brown, Joe Polish, Jeff Walker, Jack Canfield, Pat Flynn, Lisa Messenger, Chalene Johnson, Brendon Burchard, James Schramko, Taki Moore, Lisa Sasevich, Brian Tracy, Oprah – and many more!

Those family members that check in on me regularly and have been there for me, I'm so grateful to have you in my life.

All our studio owners who have joined our Association and programs... I have you to thank for being able to live each and every day doing what I love, with people I love. I'm so grateful to each of you that have joined our family of studio owners from around the world. Thank you for being you and engaging so passionately in what we're aiming to achieve in the world, which is to transform studio owners into business owners.

To the best team in the world! Bench, Mel and Cha. You are the ones who make it possible for us to impact the lives of studio owners across the globe daily. You are my family and I'm grateful to not only have you as part of my company, but also a part of my life. Thank you for the passion and persistence you bring each day! Also a big thank you to our extended team Mark, Colin, Rick, Abbey, Ed, Ashish and John, for always going above and beyond our expectations.

My amazing group of friends: Gio, Kate, Jawad, Christina, Tracy, Avigail, Katrina, Renee, Robert, Claire and Scott. Your friendship means the world to me, and I couldn't imagine my life without any of you. Thank you for being there in the great times and the challenging times. You all inspire me to be a better version of myself.

Michael, who has been my father since I was 10. I appreciate your support over the last 20 years with every endeavour I have pursued; I know you're always there and for that I'm so very thankful.

My best friend in the world and my mother – Kim. Every day, I truly feel like the luckiest child in the world to have a mother who taught me how to work hard, how to love and how to stand up for myself from a young age. Thank you for being there every step of the way – I love you more than words can say.

And lastly, my Nan, who passed away just before my 16th birthday. You have and will always be that shining light I see each morning and every night before I go to sleep. I've never forgotten your hugs, how you encouraged me to dance and to be the human being I was put on this earth to be. As a teacher, you impacted the lives of so many children that people still talk about you today. If I can make half the impact you did in this world before my time is up, then my job will be done.

Thank you also to you, the reader. I hope you have taken away at least one thing from Dance Studio Transformation that will impact your business – and your life.

To your transformation!

Clint

ABOUT THE AUTHOR – CLINT SALTER

By age 28, Clint had created, built and sold three businesses, two of them in dance. He started dancing jazz at age nine before moving on to tap, ballet and hip hop. Then, in a fortuitous turn of events, a former teacher of his sold her studio. Clint actually had parents approaching him to ask if he would teach their children — and open up his own Dance Studio. So, at the ripe age of 16, Clint and a friend started their own studio.

It started as a small studio, with just 30 students. Fast-forward five years and it was operating six days a week, with a total enrollment of a few hundred students and classes running at capacity. Clint and his partner had built a booming business — and Clint was only 21. Around that time, Clint decided to sell his half of the studio to his partner as he prepared to start working at the top celebrity agency in Australia, managing some of the biggest names in television and media.

Over the five years Clint was with the talent agency, he was responsible for pitching ideas and securing commercial endorsements, licensing, publishing, television, radio and speaking deals for his stable of high-profile clients. During this time, Clint also created DanceLife, Australia's largest community for dancers and performers. In four years of operation, DanceLife became Australia's bible of all things dance: an online resource for dancers, a large dance competition and a learn-to-dance program for primary and high schools. Clint sold DanceLife after four years to take an opportunity to be the Touring Manager for the musical *Jersey Boys*, where he travelled internationally while managing a team of 56 people.

After spending so much time working at the agency and running his businesses, Clint decided he wanted to share with dance studio owners the knowledge he'd accumulated. He wanted to help studio owners learn how to design their lives and create a thriving, profitable studio that allowed them to spend more time working 'on' rather than 'in' the business, something that is accomplished by creating a rock-solid automated business model as well as running a year-long student attraction and retention strategy. Clint is the Founder of the Dance Studio Owners Association and Studio Success Formula, the #1 Business Growth Program for dance studio owners where he offers mentoring and online training programs to help studio owners turn their passion for dance into a profitable business that makes a big difference in the lives of their dance families.

WWW.DANCESTUDIOOWNERSASSOCIATION.COM

CPSIA information can be obtained
at www.ICGtesting.com
Printed in the USA
LVHW01s2307290917
550246LV00001B/8/P